DISCARD

Lying, Cheating, and Carrying On

Margaret S. Mahler Series

This series of yearly volumes began appearing in 1991 and is based upon the panel discussions presented at the prestigious Annual Margaret Mahler Symposia held in Philadelphia. Each volume consists of three papers and their discussions presented at the most recent Symposium. A thorough introduction and a comprehensive conclusion that pulls all the material together are specially written for the book. Occasionally, one or two papers that were not presented at the meeting but represent the cutting-edge thinking on the topic are also included. While this format and organization gives these books a friendly familiarity, the books' contents vary greatly and are invariably a source of excitement and clinical enthusiasm. Volumes published so far have addressed topics as diverse as hatred and cultural differences in childhood development, extramarital affairs and sibling relationship, mourning and self psychology, and resilience and boundary violations. Among the distinguished psychoanalysts whose work has appeared in this series are Salman Akhtar, Anni Bergman, Harold Blum, Ruth Fischer, Alvin Frank, Dorothy Holmes, Otto Kernberg, Selma Kramer, Peter Neubauer, Henri Parens, Fred Pine, John Munder Ross, and Ernest Wolf, to name a few. The vantage point is always broad-based and includes developmental, clinical, and cultural variables but the end point is consistently an enhancement of the technical armamentarium of the therapist.

BOOKS BASED UPON THE MARGARET S. MAHLER SYMPOSIA

- *The Trauma of Transgression* (1991)
- *When the Body Speaks* (1992)
- *Prevention in Mental Health* (1993)
- *Mahler and Kohut* (1994)
- *The Birth of Hatred* (1995)
- *The Internal Mother* (1995)
- *Intimacy and Infidelity* (1996)
- *The Seasons of Life* (1997)
- *The Colors of Childhood* (1998)
- *Thicker Than Blood* (1999)
- *Does God Help?* (2000)
- *Three Faces of Mourning* (2001)
- *Real and Imaginary Fathers* (2004)
- *The Language of Emotions* (2005)
- *Interpersonal Boundaries* (2006)
- *Listening to Others* (2007)
- *The Unbroken Soul* (2008)
- *Lying, Cheating, and Carrying On* (2009)

Lying, Cheating, and Carrying On

*Developmental, Clinical, and
Sociocultural Aspects of Dishonesty
and Deceit*

Edited By
Salman Akhtar and Henri Parens

JASON ARONSON

Lanham • Boulder • New York • Toronto • Plymouth, UK

Published in the United States of America
by Jason Aronson
An imprint of Rowman & Littlefield Publishers, Inc.

A wholly owned subsidary of
The Rowman & Littlefield Publishing Group, Inc.
4501 Forbes Boulevard, Suite 200, Lanham, Maryland 20706
www.rowmanlittlefield.com

Estover Road
Plymouth PL6 7PY
United Kingdom

British Library Cataloguing in Publication Information Available

Library of Congress Cataloging-in-Publication Data

Lying, cheating, and carrying on : lying, cheating, and carrying on developmental,
clinical, and sociocultural aspects of dishonesty and deceit / edited by Salman Akhtar
and Henry Parens.
    p. cm. — (Margaret S. Mahler series)
    Includes bibliographical references and index.
    ISBN-13: 978-0-7657-0602-7 (cloth : alk. paper)
    ISBN-10: 0-7657-0602-4 (cloth : alk. paper)
    ISBN-13: 978-0-7657-0603-4 (pbk. : alk. paper)
    ISBN-10: 0-7657-0603-2 (pbk. : alk. paper)
    ISBN-13: 978-0-7657-0646-1 (electronic)
    ISBN-10: 0-7657-0646-6 (electronic)
    1. Truthfulness and falsehood in adolescence. I. Akhtar, Salman, 1946– II. Parens,
Henri, 1928–

BF724.3.T78L95 2009
616.85'84—dc22

                                  2008047388

Printed in the United States of America

∞™ The paper used in this publication meets the minimum requirements of
American National Standard for Information Sciences—Permanence of Paper
for Printed Library Materials, ANSI/NISO Z39.48-1992.

To

the memory of

Margaret S. Mahler and Selma Kramer

Contents

~

Acknowledgments

The chapters in this book, with the exception of chapters 1, 7, 9, and 10 were originally presented as papers at the 39th Annual Margaret S. Mahler Symposium on Child Development held on April 27, 2008. First and foremost, therefore, we wish to express our gratitude to the Department of Psychiatry of the Jefferson Medical College, the main sponsor of this event. We are especially indebted to Drs. Michael Vergare, chairman of the Department of Psychiatry and Human Behavior of the Jefferson Medical College, Bernard Freidberg, president of the Psychoanalytic Foundation of The Psychoanalytic Center of Philadelphia, and William Singletary, the president of the Margaret S. Mahler Foundation for their kind support of the Symposium. Finally, we wish to acknowledge our sincere appreciation of Ms. Melissa Nevin for her efficient organization of the symposium and for her skillful assistance in the preparation of this book's manuscript.

~

CHAPTER ONE

Lies, Liars, And Lying: An Introductory Overview

Salman Akhtar, M.D.

"Never lie in writing"
(Mason Cooley, 1992)

Borrowing a phrase from the former vice president and recent Nobel Prize winner, Al Gore, I wish to begin this discourse on lying with some 'inconvenient truths.' Here they are:

- Everyone lies.
- Anyone who claims to be forever truthful is telling a lie.
- It is undesirable to be truthful under all circumstances.
- Lying is essential for the smooth social dialogue and interpersonal politeness.
- Different forms and varying extents of lying are integral to many socially useful lines of work.
- Lying can at times save lives.
- Since all sorts of gray areas exist between what constitutes a lie and what constitutes a truth, it is not always easy to separate the two out.

It is only with the psychic ruthlessness of this backdrop that one can approach the matter of lying, cheating, and dishonesty with any modicum of seriousness. Such discussion must at its outset, address the formal characteristics of lies and the dynamic issues that propel a lie.

In the passages that follow, I will take up these issues one by one. Then I will make a brief foray into the world of forgery involving arts and antiques.

Following this sociocultural digression, I will return to the clinical realm and address the implications of lying for conducting psychotherapy and psychoanalysis. I will conclude with a few synthesizing remarks.

The Structure of a Lie

In order to grasp the various formal characteristics of a lie, it might not be out of place to begin with a simple dictionary definition. A lie, according to *Webster's Ninth Collegiate Dictionary* (1987) is "an untrue statement with intent to deceive" (p. 689). Also included in the explanatory comments that follow the initial crisp definition are phrases like "an assertion of something known or believed by the speaker to be untrue" and the deliberate creation of a "false or misleading impression" (p. 689). Pooling these tidbits with the notion of lying implicit in the well-known judicial instruction to tell "the truth, the whole truth, and nothing but the truth" leads one to the idea that a lie can be told in many ways. Lying is a multifaceted sport with diverse moves available to the deft player. Some prominent forms of lying are:

- Not telling the truth. Remaining silent while being asked to respond to a question, the answer to which one actually knows, constitutes a lie.
- Replacing the facts one knows to be true by false and misleading information
- Telling the truth but not the 'whole truth' and, by such withholding of parts of relevant information, altering the inference to be drawn from one's report.
- Telling the truth but embellishing it in a way that results in a caricature and thus puts its veracity in question. The mechanism of 'denial by exaggeration' (Fenichel, 1945) belongs in this category.
- Flatly and forcefully questioning and even repudiating an established truth. The phenomenon of 'gas lighting' (Barton and Whitehead, 1969) where one individual seeks to drive someone crazy by stirring up doubts about the latter's perception is an example of this type of lying. Instances of 'soul murder' (Shengold, 1989) where a child's perception is ruthlessly erased by cruel and abusive parent, and the denial of the Holocaust are other examples from individual and collective arenas, respectively, of this very type of lie.
- Acknowledging the truth about a certain matter but retrospectively imputing motives to it that were not in operation earlier. The ego operation of 'sliding of meanings' (Horowitz, 1975) seen in narcissistic personalities is an example par excellence of such a strategy.

What all this demonstrates is that lies come in many forms.[1] From bald-faced assertions of falsehood to subtle distortions or reality, lies elude simplistic nosological traps. To discern them, one not only requires to pay close attention to what is being said and why but also to what is not being said, what is being exaggerated, what is being minimized, and what is being painted with a revisionist brush. One also has to take into consideration the intrapsychic and interpersonal context in which a lie is being constructed and conveyed; lying invariably involves a self-object scenario, however deeply buried under narcissistic grounds that might be. And, this brings up the consideration of the motivational dynamics behind lying.

Motivation for Lying

Like all human behavior, lying is multiply-determined (Waelder, 1936). Each lie involves instinctual pressures, narcissistic interests, superego defects, and ego loopholes. Each lie is a cavern of a wishful fantasy and an attempt to ward off a dreaded imaginary scenario. Each lie constitutes a psychic maneuver to alter the self-object relations; the object involved might be a specific human being or a diffuse world of people and institutions. Each lie has origins and consequences both within the subject's psyche and his or her interpersonal surround. Each lie creates something and destroys something. Being opposed to truth, each lie, to a greater or lesser extent, attacks, or at least bypasses, the great realities of separateness, finiteness, and the ubiquitous nature of aggression, genital differences, and incest barrier.[2]

The foregoing constitutes a description of the diverse rock-bottom elements in lying. However, in a particular instance of lying, one or the other variable might play a more central role. This necessitates the distinction of motivationally different types of lies though not at the cost of overlooking their shared psychic ancestry. The following six categories readily present themselves though clearly they are not tightly exclusive and overlap each other in many ways.

- *Social lies*, which involve the innocuous excuses and pretenses of daily life.
- *Narcissistic lies*, which include omissions and exaggerations for avoiding shame.
- *Psychopathic lies* or deliberate misrepresentations aimed at obtaining material or sensual gratification.
- *Pathological lies*, which betray a pervasive inability to tell the truth arising out of an early and fundamental hatred of reality.

- *Life saving lies,* which have to be spoken in situations of being held hostage or tortured.
- *Occupational lies* or deceits that are integral to being a spy or undercover agent.

Within psychoanalysis, Wilfred Bion (1970) has given most thought to this topic, looking at the pathological as well as creative aspects of lying. Bion concluded that truth, being self-evident, does not require a thinker but a lie, being a manufactured thought, does. Lemma (2005) has also made a significant contribution to the psychoanalytic understanding of lying. According to her, there are three psychic and relational configurations associated with lying: (1) *sadistic lying* where the object is duped in an effort to reverse earlier humiliations of the self, (2) *self-preservative lying* where an embellished picture of the self is offered in order to seduce someone perceived to be disinterested, and (3) a different form of self-preservative lying which could be called *self-protective lying* (though Lemma herself does not employ this expression) and is intended to protect oneself from an intrusive object.[3]

Two other issues need mention. The collapse of motivation and consequence in lying (e.g., shame leading to lying and this resulting in a deceived other party) is at times obvious. At other times, there occur consequences that were not motivationally sought (e.g., shame leading to lying resulting in an awful feeling of guilt at having misled someone). In other words, the consequences of lying are both the desired one and the undesired ones and both types of consequences might involve the self and other. A parallel concern is the psychology of one who is lied to. While unconscious collusion might exist between him and the liar, the individual who is fooled brings his own dynamics to the situation. He might be unduly gullible and believe all that is told to him though not without feeling deceived and hurt later on. Curiously, some paranoid personalities—while contemptuous of others' naiveté—are themselves remarkably, though latently, gullible (Stanton, 1978).

The second point to be noted is while individual lying is largely viewed as pathological, socially sanctioned forms of lying—or certainly telling less than the whole truth or distorting the truth—form the operational backbone of many professions. One look at the meticulously doctored ads in a fashion magazine, a few minutes of listening to a used car salesman, a glimpse at the 'true revelations' by a tabloid journalist, the partaking of a political spinmeister's rhetoric, and the innocent belief in the declarations by national leaders[4] will convince anyone of this assertion. Such societal lies may result in the relatively harmless seduction to purchase this or that cosmetic or perfume. Or, they might have a devastating impact on individuals and families; the 'liar loans' (Zibel, 2008)—home mortgages approved without checking the borrower's income or assets—and the notorious Enron scandal that decimated the financial security of hundreds of people illustrate this quite well. Needless to say, however, reactions to such lies vary greatly ranging from amused disbelief through pain and disgust to intense moral outrage. Nowhere is this drama played with more cleverness and intrigue than in the marketplace of arts and antiques.

The World of Forgery

Forgers and counterfeiters who claim to have "discovered" amazing antiquities and 'created' great pieces of art exist worldwide. In the fascinating accounts of their 'accomplishments,' consideration of their motives gets lost. What makes them do it? What makes anyone pass off an inauthentic product as authentic? Why do people cheat? One the surface, the answer to such questions is simple. One look at the exorbitant prices successful forgeries in the realm of art can fetch and you know that monetary benefit is a major motivation for such "creativity of deception." It ought to be noted though that before art became commercialized, reproducing the work of a master was considered a sign of respect, not a forgery. Copies were recognized as such and financial gain did not motivate their production. It is with the Renaissance, when the interest in cultural antiquities raised the monetary value of art, that the trend toward passing off such 'copies' as real began. There was money to be made by such forgery.

The list of those who thrive in this business is indeed long. Two outstanding art forgers who made enormous money by their deceptive craft are Hans van Meegeren (1889–1947), the Dutch art dealer who painted many fake Vermeers, and Tom Keating (1917–1984), the British con artist who forged more than two thousand paintings by more than one hundred artists in his lifetime. The fact, however, is that the money made by these two master forgers constitutes a minuscule proportion of that made by art forgers all over the world. And art is not the only arena where fake products offer lucrative financial rewards. Collectors of autographs, rare manuscripts, old photographs, letters, and even stamps and coins know very well how widely inauthentic objects circulate in the bazaars of their passion. They can readily recount all sorts of tales involving someone being swindled by a forger who got away with a huge sum of money.

However, monetary profit is not the only motive for creating a forgery. Emotional factors also seem to play a role here. Prominent among these are the following:

- Creating a 'successful' forgery affords one the wicked pleasure of fooling others. Compared to oneself, others now appear silly and stupid. The sadistic triumph over their innocence results in gleeful mocking on a secret basis. It promises to undo the chronic feelings of inferiority and impotence the forger often carries within himself.
- Trading in fake products invariably involves a rebellion against ordinary morality. It involves breaking the law as well. Making and selling counterfeit objects can thus give vent to emotional conflicts with authority figures. The irreverence and bravado of an imposter is a slap in the face of the established order. The ever-present risk of being caught adds to the thrill of defiance.
- Fakery also fulfills strivings for magical powers. To produce a dollar bill in one's basement, for instance, gratifies our childish wishes for becoming 'rich' pronto. To paint a Cezanne or a Picasso over a few days in downtown Cleveland is to reverse time, change location, and acquire creative genius at will. Just like that, with a snap of the fingers.

Such considerations of the forger's sentiments bring us to the other side of the equation, namely the emotional responses of the witness of a forgery. As victims of forgery, we feel an admixture of outrage and shame. We are hurt by the betrayal and embarrassed by our gullibility. Interestingly even when we are mere witnesses or onlookers of a forgery, not its victim, our responses are not simple.

We are all familiar with the scorn we feel upon seeing poorly made Barbie dolls from the Persian Gulf, French perfumes concocted in the Philippines, faux-pearl necklaces offered on QVC, fake Rolex watches sold on a street corner, Coach handbags made in Guatemala, and designer-label clothing made in Bangladeshi sweatshops. We deride them. The scorn reflects our rejection of fraudulence in general. It helps us repudiate aspects of inauthenticity in our own personality makeup. It is as if by belittling fake products we are saying that we ourselves are entirely genuine in our day-to-day behavior. Our dislike of counterfeit goods thus turns out to be rather self-serving. This is a sort of fakery itself.

More embarrassing is the possibility that forgeries and counterfeit products provide vicarious gratification of our hidden, less-than-noble impulses. The childhood intolerance for the labor of effort and for the helplessness of waiting to become adept at something finds a secret ally in the producer of artifice. He fuels our suppressed longings for quick and swift results that are achieved without effort and practice. He tells us that the omnipotence we have reluctantly renounced can find gratification after all. He offers us a path that does not traverse through law-abiding territories of learning, practice, and hard work. And we gladly give in to his seductions. To put it bluntly, the clandestine pact between us and the forger goes like this: "If this guy in Texas can paint a Van Gogh, maybe we too can accomplish great and even impossible feats. If he can break rules and fool others, maybe we can also do that which is prohibited to us." No wonder we feel a mixture of barely suppressed thrill and a delicious wave of guilty fear upon encountering a fake product. Hold a counterfeit hundred-dollar bill in your hands and you will immediately know what I am talking about.

Something even deeper about human nature is revealed by the observation that we admire a better fake more than a sloppy fake. The more devilishly fooled we are, the more delight we take in the impostor's product. Why is that? Is the pleasure offered us by a good fake merely aesthetic? In other words, do we like a better replica of Rodin's *The Thinker* or of the Leaning Tower of Pisa because they look good, that is, closer to the original thing? Or is it because the better-executed fake shows more thoughtfulness and effort and, by implication, a greater amount of respect toward the creator of the original? The answer to both of these questions is a resounding yes. Overtly, our reasons for reacting more favorably to a good fake are aesthetic. A replica that closely approximates the original stimulates the admiration we feel toward the latter. We like the sensation. Covertly, witnessing a good fake provides us a well-balanced compromise between our longings for magic on the one hand and the recognition of value of effort on the other. It also provides a simultaneous gratification of our childhood wishes to outsmart our parents as well as keep them on a higher level than us, and since all of us have the remnants of such childhood wishes in the basement of our minds, it is not surprising that we simply 'love' a well-executed fake.

Back to a Clinical Realm

Encounters with deceitful patients, especially those with prominent antisocial features, makes one painfully aware of the limits of the applicability of psychoanalysis and even psychoanalytic psychotherapy (Stone, 2007). Freud's (1905) declaration that in order to tolerate the rigors of psychoanalytic treatment, one must possess "a fairly reliable character" (p. 263) readily comes to mind in this context. Without honest self-revelation, or at least the intent for it, the therapeutic alliance remains a sham. Gross psychopaths are therefore not suitable subjects for psychoanalytically derived therapies. Those with milder antisocial tendencies can, at times, benefit from such treatment especially when confrontational and cognitive-behavioral interventions are used in conjunction with it (Kernberg, 1984, 1992; Cloninger, 2005; Stone, 2007).

Such work might have to start from the very first session of the patient's evaluation. The discovery of an overt disregard for the basic conditions of treatment (e.g., refusing to tell one's real name or to give proper contact information) and outright lying needs to be immediately confronted. Prospect for future therapy is better if such confrontation leads to plausible explanations (e.g., the patient's need to conceal his identity because he's in a government witness protection program) or anxiety and shame leading to a quick rectification of the earlier misstatement. If, however, the patient responds to the confrontation by more lies, improbable rationalizations, argumentativeness, and rage, the prognosis is guarded (Akhtar, 1992). Under such circumstances it might not even be possible to begin a treatment. "Therapists who believe that with enough effort, they can make every patient stay the course are engaging in omnipotence" (Yeomans et al., 1992, p. 9).

The discovery of deceitfulness might be made much later in the encounter with less psychopathic individuals. Lies, distortions of truth, and deliberate withholding of information might enter the treatment as a form of narcissistic resistance and a ploy to keep one's shame-laden aspects hidden from the therapist. Such self-protective motivations might extend to warding off castration anxiety by repudiating assertive authenticity (Gediman, 1985) and keeping in abeyance fears that one would not be liked for what one is in reality (Lemma, 2005). On the other hand, lying may have greater discharge functions related to early object relations. Falsehood then itself becomes a form of transference relatedness. Here Kernberg's (1992) concept of *psychopathic transference* is pertinent. According to him, a patient in the throes of such transference consistently lies to the therapist, suppresses useful information, and, as a result of projecting his own corrupt tendencies, believes that the therapist is dishonest and untrustworthy. At times, the patient tries "unconsciously to provoke the therapist to deceptive or dishonest behavior, or at least to inconsistencies in his behavior that the patient may then interpret as dishonesty" (p. 223). Kernberg proposes that the proper approach under such circumstances is to confront the patient tactfully but directly and to explore the inherent transference relationship in detail and to resolve it interpretively before proceeding with other issues. Typically, the 'psychopathic transference' gets transformed into 'paranoid transference' before giving way to depressive reparative feelings and genuine self-concern.

In extending Kernberg's work, LaFarge (1995) described three transferences characteristic of patients in whom deception and inauthenticity are organizing themes: (1) *imposturous transference* in which the patient actively enjoys deceiving the analyst by his fabrications; (2) *psychopathic-paranoid transference* in which the patient is intensely involved with the analyst who he feels is lying to him and will betray him; and (3) the *psychopathic-unreal transference* in which the patient feels disconnected with the analyst and automaton-like in his own experience. LaFarge goes on to suggest that two kinds of splitting are evident in these patients. The first is a compartmentalization of self-and object-representations along the libidinal and aggressive lines. The second is a schism in the experience of reality, with some self-and object-representations felt to be exaggeratedly and painfully real and others felt to be lifeless and devoid of meaning. LaFarge indicates that the two psychopathic configurations are dissociated halves of a single bad self-and object relations. Each of this unit is used defensively against the full experience of complex but frustrated object relations. Moreover, each dissociated system incorporates a central fantasy of the parent-child relationship, which comes to acquire determinants and functions from successive developmental levels.

The imposturous transference is at a somewhat higher level. It is derived from an identification, especially in the male patients (who show it more often), with a grandiose representation of the father in order to patch over a defective body representation that is poorly differentiated from that of the mother. The imposturous transference can serve as a psychostructural umbrella for the psychopathic transferences and the latter can emerge as regressive defenses when oedipal guilt and castration anxiety render the imposturous tendency too risky.

Mention must also be made of O'Shaughnessy's (1990) elegant and thoughtful paper titled "Can a liar be psychoanalyzed?" Underscoring the "fundamental antagonism between a liar and a psychoanalyst" (p. 187), O'Shaughnessy described two cases in detail which are quite similar to those included in the paper by LaFarge (1995) mentioned above. Both were males[5]. Both lied with excitement initially and then turned paranoid. Both had "basic suspicions" (p. 190) instead of basic trust and both felt "cut off from their depths" (p. 191). Like LaFarge, O'Shaughnessy observed the imposters tendency toward idealization: "This lie about lying is at the center of the deterioration of his character" (p. 193). O'Shaughnessy delineated the characteristic "triad of a deficient primal object, a strong destructive instinct in the patient, and a general perverse overlay"

(p. 193) in such situations. Her conclusion that if all three aspects can (identification with a lying object, hostility, and perverse delight) be addressed, a genuine psychoanalytic process can be set into motion paralleled Kernberg's (1992) and LaFarge's (1995) proposals.

A special challenge is posed by patients who keep secrets. A secret is "an intrapsychic cul-de-sac which not only disrupts life's experiential continuity but also sets into motion defensive processes to guard its own existence" (Akhtar, 1985, p. 82). While psychoanalysts regularly hear material that their patients wish to keep secret from others and gradually discern the secrets of the child within these patients (Gross, 1951; Sulzberger, 1953), encountering patients who tenaciously withhold pockets of information is disconcerting to them. The risk of countertransference outrage and intrusiveness is great under such circumstances. While no hard and fast rule can be set, keeping the following guidelines might be helpful. When secrets betray split-off sectors of personality and secret keeping has instinctual discharge function (e.g., teasing, exclusion, and sadism), then a confrontative-interpretative approach seems better. When secrets are kept predominantly as a defense (e.g., against shame) and the act of secret keeping has symbolic significance, the traditional, slow, step-by-step approach centering upon defense interpretation is more useful. Kernberg's (1984, 1992) and Margolis's (1966, 1974) contributions are especially instructive in the former and latter regards, respectively.

Such emphasis upon the interpretive approach must not overshadow the importance of the analyst's 'holding' (Winnicott, 1960) functions and of his capacity to discern unconscious hope (that the environment will tolerate the burden of deceit and yet continue to provide care) in the patient's cheating and outrageousness (Winnicott, 1956).[6] Only with such a judicious and tactful admixture of holding and interpretive approaches and that too on a sustained and long-term basis can a liar be truly helped.

An Ancient Indian Parable in Conclusion

In this wide-ranging survey, I have delineated the formal characteristics of lies, phenomenological subtypes of lies, and psychodynamic motivations to distort the known truth. Utilizing the scene of art forgery as a didactic scaffold, I have elucidated the dialectical configurations that intricately bind the liar and his victim. Such a 'two-person' explanatory approach has, however, not stood in my way to recognize the truly 'one-person' contributions to the phenomenon of lying. My emphasis has overall been on the multiply determined, multi-functional, object-related, and ubiquitous nature of lying. At the same time, I have emphasized that a concerted effort to be honest and seek psychic truth—to the extent any such striving can be fully successful—is a fundamental aspect of mental health and of intensive psychotherapy and psychoanalysis.[7] With this in mind, I have made brief comments on patients who misinform their therapists during the initial evaluation, the development of psychopathic transferences, and the special case of secret keeping that invariably complicates the progress of treatment.

I would like to conclude with a parable drawn from *Panchtantra*, the ancient Indian book of folk tales (circa third century B.C.). The tale goes like this. Once a woodsman was going through a jungle where he came across a lion trapped inside an iron cage. The lion is understandably upset and upon seeing the woodsman urges him to open the gate of the cage and release him. The woodsman does not appear keen on this since he feels afraid of the beast; indeed he fears that the lion will eat him up upon being released. However, when he voices his concern, the lion emphatically assures him that he would do no such thing. The lion says that he would be utterly grateful and cannot conceive of attacking someone who saved his life. Finding the lion to be earnest, the woodsman opens the cage and the lion comes out. Moments later, the lion tells the woodsman that he wants to eat him up. The woodsman is dismayed and reminds the lion of his promise not to do so. The lion says that he was telling the truth when he promised but the procrastination on the woodsman's part to release him caused delay and this, in turn, made him hungry. He says that now he cannot help himself and has to eat the woodsman. Just as this discussion is going on, a jackal happens to pass by. He stops and asks the arguing duo what is going on. Upon being told the story, first by the woodsman and then by the lion, with their obvious mismatch, the jackal turns pensive. He thinks for a while and then says that he does not believe either of them. In fact, he calls both the woodsman and the lion liars. He says that he cannot believe that such a large and majestic animal like the lion could ever fit in that small iron cage. He mocks the woodsman and the lion for fabricating such an incredible tale. Annoyed at this, the lion promptly decides to prove the jackal wrong and reenters the cage. With lightning speed, the jackal locks the cage door and thus saves the woodsman's life.

As one encounters a fable of such richness, many questions present themselves.

- Was the lion telling the truth when he said to the woodsman that he would not attack him?
- Was the lion lying when he said that his hunger had grown because of the woodman's procrastination?

- Was the woodsman pathologically gullible (due perhaps to some unconscious masochism) in trusting the lion to begin with?
- Was the jackal truthful when he accused the lion and the woodsman of being liars?
- Was the lion pathologically gullible (due to his unconscious guilt at cheating the woodsman) to believe the jackal and reenter the cage?
- Was the woodsman aware of the jackal's lying and in remaining silent about it, was he not lying himself?

Such questions—and I am certain that many more like these can be raised—underscore the gray areas between truth and lie, the importance of the perspective from which a particular statement is assessed, the moral dilemmas inherent in making judgments in this realm, and ultimately, the object relational and intersubjective context of lies and lying. These questions are therefore important. However, the richness of texture they provide should not be exploited in the service of moral skepticism. The existence of complexity in this realm does not mean that there is no such thing as objective truth. Indeed, there is. The fact that you are reading these words (regardless if you agree or disagree with them) is one such truth and to deny it would be a lie.

Notes

1. Any discussion of lies contains within itself implicit assumptions about truth. If it were not so and truth did not exist (or, was not known), how could anything be considered a lie? In other words, to know a lie is to know the truth behind its veil. This theorem might not fit well with the contemporary hermeneutic turn to psychoanalysis, which lays emphasis upon co-constructed data, intersubjectivity, and 'narrative truth' (Spence, 1982). Sass and Woolfolk (1988) have provided a thorough assessment of this tension and Hanly (1990, 1992) has elucidated the criteria (e.g., coherence, correspondence) for establishing 'truth' in psychoanalysis.

2. Chasseguet-Smirgel's (1984) concept of regressive anal homogenization in the perverse character and Grunberger's (1989) metapsychological discourse on the false notion of 'purity' are especially pertinent in this context.

3. In the preoccupation with delineating different types of lies, it should not be overlooked that inability to lie, when circumstances demand such a posture, might also reflect psychopathology. Such 'compulsive honesty' (Rajnish Mago, personal communication, August, 19, 2008) is often accompanied by self-glorification, moralistic exaltation of truth for its own sake, and a sadomasochistic bent to interpersonal relationships. In more severe cases, such driven desire to be 'honest' is coupled with a split-off sector of personality that may be quite corrupt and perverse.

4. A thorough account of lies told by United States presidents to Congress, the media, and the public-at-large is provided by Alterman (2004). It is a painful saga of how moral values and the honorable covenant to uphold the truth at the highest level of a democratic government can get sacrificed at the altar of political convenience. While Bill Clinton's bald faced denial ("I did not have sex with that woman, Miss Lewinsky") has its titillating impact, far more serious consequences have followed Lyndon Johnson's deceptive assurances regarding the second Tonkin Gulf incident, Richard Nixon's Watergate cover-up, Ronald Reagan's lies regarding the Iran-Contra deal, George H.W. Bush false promises ("read my lips: no new taxes"), and George W. Bush's fabricated reasons to attack Iraq. Indeed hundreds of thousands of people have been killed because of the last mentioned deceit not to mention its devastating impact upon the American economy and the nation's prestige in the eyes of the world.

5. Actually most lying patients reported in psychoanalytic literature are male. This could be due in part to the greater prevalence of antisocial traits among men (Cloninger et al., 1975; DSM-IV, 1990). What is more curious, however, is that a disproportionate number of papers on lying are written by female analysts (Deutsch, 1922; Greenacre, 1958; Olden, 1941; Chassegeut-Smirgel, 1984; LaFarge, 1995; Lemma, 2005); a few contributions by male analysts (Abraham, 1925; Blum, 1983; Kernberg, 1992) paradoxically support the female authorial dominance in this realm. The reasons for this are, however, unclear. Could it be that female analysts are better at detecting lies told by analysands? Or, is it that deceitful men deliberately seek women analysts? The latter hypothesis finds support in Chasseguet-Smirgel's (1984) observation that male fraudulence grows out of maternal seduction and the resulting inability to fully experience the oedipal situation. Perhaps imposturous men seek female analysts to avoid passive homosexual urges and unconscious guilt vis-à-vis the father whom they have by-passed and intrapsychically killed.

6. Abraham's (1925) psychoanalytically informed account of a chronic swindler's life with its unexpectedly good outcome underscores the potentially redeeming role of forebearance vis-a-vis such psychopathology.

7. The psychoanalytic emphasis upon truth, truthfulness, and truth-seeking should, however, not lead to idealizing psychoanalysts. Knowledgeable though they might be about the matters of mind, psychoanalysts are nonetheless ordinary human beings. Like others, they have character flaws and vulnerabilities. They are hardly immune to the temptations of lying. Sigmund Freud's signing "Dr. Sigm Freud u frau" (German for Dr. Sigmund Freud and wife) when he checked into a hotel in Maloja, Switzerland on August 13, 1898 accompanied by his sister-in-law Minna Bernays (Blumenthal, 2006) is a recently unearthed piece of psychoanalytic history that supports this assertion. Other prominent examples are Wilhelm Stekel's fabricating clinical material for presentations at early gatherings at Freud's house (Bos and Groenendijk, 2006), Masud Khan's merrily declaring himself to be a 'Prince' (Hopkins, 2006; Akhtar, 2007), and Heinz Kohut's (1979) report on the

'two analyses of Mr. Z' which in fact was an "appalling deception" (Giovachinni, 2000, p. 78) since Mr. Z was most likely Kohut himself and there had been no second analysis (see also Strozier 2004).

References

Abraham, K. (1925). The history of an impostor in the light of psychoanalytic knowledge. In: *Clinical Papers and Essays on Psychoanalysis* (pp. 291–305). New York: Brunner–Mazel, 1958.

Akhtar, S. (1985). The other woman: phenomenological, psychodynamic, and therapeutic considerations. In: *Contemporary Marriage*, ed. D. Goldberg, pp. 215–240. Homeswood, IL: Dow Jones–Irwin

Akhtar, S. (1992). *Broken Structures: Severe Personality Disorders and Their Treatment.* Northvale, NJ: Jason Aronson.

Akhtar, S. (2007a). *Regarding Others: Reviews, Responses, and Reflections*, pp. 80–84. Charlottesville, VA: Pitchstone Publishing.

Akhtar, S. (2007b). Four roadblocks in approaching Masud Khan. *Psychoanalytic Quarterly* 76: 991–995.

Alterman, E. (2004). When presidents lie. *The Nation*, October 5, 2004.

Barton, R. and Whitehead, J. (1969). The gaslight phenomenon. *Lancet* 1: 1258–1260.

Bion, W. (1970). Lies and the thinker. In: *Attention and Interpretation.* London: Tavistock.

Blum, H. (1983). The psychoanalytic process and psychoanalytic inference: a clinical study of a lie and a loss. *International Journal of Psychoanalysis* 64: 7–33.

Blumenthal, R. (2006). Hotel log hints at illicit desire that Dr. Freud did not repress. *The New York Times*, p. A1, December 24.

Bos, J. and Groenendijk, L. (2006). *The Self-Marginalization of Wilhelm Stekel: Freudian Circles Inside and Out.* New York: Springer.

Celenza, A. (2006). *Sexual Boundary Violations: Therapeutic, Supervisory, and Academic Contexts.* Lanham, MD: Jason Aronson.

Chasseguet-Smirgel, J. (1984). *Creativity and Perversion.* New York: W.W. Norton.

Cloninger, C.R. (2005). Antisocial personality disorder: a review. In: *Personality Disorders*, eds. M. Maj, H. Akiskal, J. Mezzich, and A. Okasha, pp. 125–169. Chichester, UK: John Wiley & Sons.

Cloninger, C.R., Reich, T., and Guze, S.B. (1975). The multifactorial model of disease transmission II: sex differences in the familial transmission of sociopathy (antisocial personality). *British Journal of Psychiatry* 127: 11–22.

Cooley, M. (1992). *City Aphorisms*, Ninth Selection. New York: Grove Press.

Deutsch, H. (1922). On the pathological lie. *Journal of the American Academy of Psychoanalysis* 10: 386–396, reprinted, 1982.

Fenichel, O. (1945). *The Psychoanalytic Theory of Neurosis.* New York: W.W. Norton.

Freud, S. (1905). On psychotherapy. *Standard Edition* 7: 257–268.

Gediman, H. (1985). Impostor, inauthenticity, and feeling fraudulent. *Journal of the American Psychoanalytic Association* 39: 911–936.

Giovacchini, P. (2000). *Impact of Narcissism: The Errant Therapist in a Chaotic Quest*. Northvale, NJ: Jason Aronson.

Gross, A. (1951). The secret. *Bulletin of the Menninger Clinic* 15: 37–44.

Grunberger, B. (1989). *New Essays on Narcissism* (D. Macey, Trans.). London: Free Association Books.

Hanly, C. (1990). The concept of truth and psychoanalysis. *International Journal of Psychoanalysis* 71: 375–384.

Hanly, C. (1992). *The Problem With Truth in Applied Psychoanalysis*. New York: Guilford Press.

Hopkins, L. (2006). *False Self: The Life of Masud Khan*. New York: The Other Press.

Kernberg, O.F. (1984). *Severe Personality Disorders: Psychotherapeutic Strategies*. New Haven, CT: Yale University Press.

Kernberg, O.F. (1992). *Aggression in Personality Disorders and Perversions*. New Haven, CT: Yale University Press.

Klein, M. (1946). Notes on some schizoid mechanisms. In: *Envy and Gratitude and Other Works—1946–1963*. New York: Free Press, 1975.

LaFarge, L. (1995). Transferences of deception. *Journal of the American Psychoanalytic Association* 48: 765–792.

Lemma, A. (2005). The many faces of lying. *International Journal of Psychoanalysis* 86: 737–753.

Margolis, G. (1966). Secrecy and identity. *International Review of Psychoanalysis* 47:517–522.

Margolis, G. (1974). The psychology of keeping secrets. *International Journal of Psychoanalysis* 1: 291–296.

Olden, C. (1941). About the fascinating effect of the narcissistic personality. *American Imago* 2: 347–355.

O' Shaughnessy, E. (1990). Can a liar be psychoanalyzed? *International Journal of Psychoanalysis* 71:187–196.

Sass, L. and Woolfork, R. (1988). Psychoanalysis and the hermeneutic turn: a critique of 'narrative truth and historical truth.' *Journal of the American Psychoanalytic Association* 36: 429–454.

Shengold, L. (1989). *Soul Murder*. New Haven, CT: Yale University Press.

Spence, D. (1982). Narrative truth and historical truth. *Psychoanalytic Quarterly* 51:43–61.

Stanton, A.H. (1978). Personality disorders. In: *The Harvard Guide to Modern Psychiatry*, ed. A.M. Nicoli, pp. 283–295. Cambridge, MA: Belknap Press.

Stone, M. (2007). Treatability in severe personality disorders: how far do the science and art of psychotherapy carry us? In: *Severe Personality Disorders: Everyday Issues in Clinical Practice*, eds. B. van Luyn, S. Akthar, and W.J. Livesley, pp. 1–29. Cambridge, UK: Cambridge University Press.

Strozier, C. (2004). *Heinz Kohut: The Making of a Psychoanalyst.* New York: Other Press.

Sulzberger, C. (1953). Why it is hard to keep secrets. *Psychoanalysis* 2: 37–43.

Webster's Ninth New Collegiate Dictionary (1987). Springfield, MA: Merriam-Webster Inc.

Yeomans, F., Selzer, M., and Clarkin, J. (1992). *Treating the Borderline Patient: A Contract Based Approach.* New York: Basic Books.

Zibel, A. (2008). Truth time: lenders are about to pay the price for handing out 'liar loans.' *The Philadelphia Inquirer*, p. C1, August 19.

CHAPTER TWO

What it Takes to Tell a Lie

Ruth M. S. Fischer, M.D.

"Tobias Wolff's characters are compulsive storytellers and liars; they are constantly spinning their own lives into melodramas, inventing or embellishing personas, daydreaming themselves into fantasy worlds, or turning their pasts into confessional anecdotes. Some embroider the truth to try to make themselves seem more interesting. Some lie out of self-delusion. Some invent phony identities so that they can cheat strangers out of money. Some fantasize as an escape from the banality of their lives. In Mr. Wolff's hands their story telling becomes a metaphor both for people's need to make narrative order out of the chaos of daily existence and for the fiction-making process he practices himself" (Kakutani, 2008, p. 34).

Lying or embellishing the truth has many origins and demands multiple capabilities. My focus is on the developmental attainments required to be able to deceive. Celia, age two, awoke from her nap and announced, "no poopy," denying the presence of a very obvious dirty diaper. Danny, at four, ran down the beach with a towel tied around his neck, claiming to be Superman. Alex, a first grader, stating that she knows algebra, writes down random numbers telling me that I just don't understand such difficult problems, and Peter, an adolescent, denies taking drugs in spite of all the evidence to the contrary. Ms. A., when advised to freely associate assiduously avoids certain topics and affects preferring to hold on to an important false idea rather than explore and discover some unwanted truth. Lying is defined as deceitfulness, the intentional use of lies, untruthfulness, intent to mislead or be fraudulent, not telling the whole truth. Then these all qualify as lies. But, do they?

I understand lying to be a developmental achievement. Before one can lie one must have acquired a profound level of cognitive and emotional development. So, my focus is on the question of when it is that children are developmentally capable of lying and what are the intrapsychic capacities required for the formation of a lie.

In true psychoanalytic fashion, I begin with Freud. The first reference to lying in the psychoanalytic literature occurs in the case of Little Hans (Freud, 1909). This is the case that Freud used to validate his ideas of the oedipal complex, noted in the free associations of adults and now noted as it develops and is expressed by a child. This is also the beginning of infant observation and child analysis. Freud had knowledge of Hans between the ages of two and a half and four by way of reports from the father. What began as an effort to accumulate data about normal child development became a chance to observe a reaction to the birth of a sibling and then, a little over one year later, the development and resolution of a symptom, Hans' phobia. Recently, this case has been reconsidered in light of new information about the family situation (Blum, 2007). For our purposes, however, this case is of interest as it gives us the first reference to lying. In it Hans relates in detail how Hanna had lived with the family at Gmunden the summer before her birth, of how she had traveled there with the family and of all that she had been capable of doing at that time (Freud, 1909, p. 69). Freud notes, "the effrontery with which Hans related the fantasy and the 'countless extravagant lies' with which he interwove it" (Freud, 1909, p. 129). The lying was understood as "revenge upon his father against whom he harbored a grudge for having misled him with the stork fable. It was just as though he had meant to say, 'If you really thought I was stupid as all that and expected me to believe that the stork brought Hanna, then in return I expect you to accept my invention as truth'"(Freud, 1909, p. 129).

The lie was understood to be a turning around of the narcissistic injury resulting from the lie and from the betrayal. It was revenge against the father who had lied to him about his mother's pregnancy and delivery via the stork (Freud, 1909 p. 70). In a later reference, Freud (1913) notes that children lie in identification with adults who lie to them. Kohut (1971) connected lying with narcissistic disturbances. Weinshel (1979) stressed the communicative aspect and understood it as an attempt at recreating a feeling of infantile omnipotence achieved when others accepted the lies. Greenacre (1958), suggested that those who believed the lies had an unconscious need to share in the omnipotence. More recent attention to lying is noted in an article by

Wilkinson and Hough (1996), who wrote of two abused, neglected adolescents whose lies were understood to express their fragmented self and object representations, as well as to be an expression of a narrative truth and an attempt to repair early trauma.

Since Freud, we have directed our efforts toward understanding the motivation for the lying in addition to the meanings embedded in it. There is one outstanding exception to this and that is a recent article by Halpert (2000) in which he considers the developmental requirements for lying. It is this line of thought that I will explore and expand upon.

Seven Intrapsychic Capacities Required to Lie

If I were to list the intrapsychic capabilities required to lie, it would include the establishment of an attachment bond that allows for both a sense of oneness and separateness, the ability to separate out self from other, the rapprochement subphase, Tyson's representational object constancy (Tyson, 1996), reflective functioning (Fonagy, 2001), promoting a differentiation of reality from fantasy and the integration of the psychic equivalence and pretend modes of functioning, the attainment of a certain level of cognitive development and affective containment and the all important ability to play. I will review and expound upon each of these capacities as I proceed.

Establishment of Attachment

We begin with the attachment experience about which there has been much current interest. Psychoanalysis has learned a great deal and incorporated many ideas from attachment theorists, neurobiologists, and infant researchers. However, these are not totally new ideas as many renowned psychoanalysts, Spitz (1965), Winnicott (1965), Anna Freud (1944, 1941–1945), Fraiberg (1987), Mahler (1976), and more recently Stern (1985), Emde (1980), and Fonagy and Target (1996) have concerned themselves extensively with this topic.

Neurobiology, cognitive science and attachment theory all focus on the importance of establishing, in the earliest stages of life, a solid, safe, secure bond so that developmental progress proceeds normally. The quality of the early attachment profoundly influences both neurotransmitter production controlling anxiety regulation and maturation of the infant's right brain stress coping systems, especially the amygdala and the orbito-frontal cortex (Schore, 1997). The mother's presence serves as the regulator of this basic physiological system impacting affect regulation, impulse control, and ability to concentrate. With secure attachment, the right brain emotion processing synchronizes energy flows between the infant's and the mother's brain (Schore, 1994, 2002, Slade, 1999, Gergely and Watson, 1996, Fonagy, 2003, Lyons-Ruth, 2006). The emotional resonance normally experienced in the parent infant relationship might possibly be replicated in the psychoanalytic relationship restoring right hemisphere activity lost or not adequately developed in early childhood.

Demarcation of Self and Other

Mahler (1976) understood the child to gradually separate out from a sense of oneness with mother to develop an internal representation of a clearer, more boundaried sense of self and other. Although Mahler's ideas about the earliest autistic and symbiotic phases have been seriously questioned (Pine, 2004), they do draw our attention to the early attachment experience. We no longer think of an autistic shell or a total enmeshment of infant and parent but we are increasingly aware of the dyadic interaction, the resonance, the attunement in the relationship and of its overriding importance in the child's developmental trajectory. We now appreciate the infant's more independent center of initiative and responsiveness than that which Mahler originally postulated. At the same time, we are focusing with greater interest and intensity on the very mother infant interaction that was central to her work.

Mahler (1976) approached the problem from both inside and outside of the child: the maturational unfolding from within and the external interaction with the mother from without, the two processes interacting with and enhancing each other. The internal unfolding allows for the development of the bond and then promotes the separating and individuating out from within the bond, the differentiation, practicing, rapprochement sub-phases leading to the 'on the way to object constancy' subphase, in which there is the establishment of a stable internal representation of self and other and self with other.

The contribution of the environment, the relationship the child has with the mother, is the context in which the unfolding takes place. Mahler was pointing the way to the important role the mother plays in this process. She appreciated the two-way interaction that ensues between the mother and her developing infant. Her ideas, built solidly on her forebears, pointed the way to our current interest in attachment, intersubjectivity and close processing of interaction.

Winnicott's concepts of the maturational process and the facilitating environment (1965), 'there is no such thing as a baby' and the 'ordinary devoted mother' closely relate to Mahler's two-fold focus on the contributions of the infant and of the mother. In considering the 'good-enough mother,' Winnicott makes the analogy of planting a bulb. With the right kind of earth and water, the bulb grows into a daffodil as it has its own vital spark, the maturational unfolding, and has had a good enough environment. Mahler writes of the infant's maturation within the interaction of constitution, the vital spark, and the relationship, the contribution of the environment. Both Mahler and Winnicott emphasize the interaction. One cannot grow without the outer sustenance but there must not be too great an impingement of external reality on the infant's inner core or growth will be stunted.

The development of the true self (1965), a Winnicottian concept, must be introduced at this juncture. That which is real, true, and authentic within the child develops as the result of the mother's ability to recognize the infant as real and separate. Her capacity to know, represent, and reflect the infant's experience back to him is intrinsic to the establishment of this sense of realness, of a true self, of object- and self-constancy as well as the infant's capacity to represent and later symbolize his inner life. The mother provides the means for the child coming to know and represent his own experience. This is the mother of the differentiation subphase who delights in the child's exploration of her face, glasses, and jewelry and the mother of the practicing subphase who enjoys her child's newfound motoric capabilities and forays into the world as well as the mother of the rapprochement who contains the conflict of autonomy and closeness. Denial or lack of validation of that which is experienced leads to the development of a false self, an inability to truly know oneself and another, and ultimately to a sense of inauthenticity.

Successful Negotiation of the Rapprochement Subphase

In more current parlance, we speak of the parent mirroring and marking the infant's experience as a way for the child to recognize what is being experienced (Gergely and Watson, 1996). The child's sadness, anger and joy are reflected back to the child in the parent's face, tone, and posture, but not in exact replica. Rather it is marked, exaggerated, or modified so that it is recognized, contained, and played with. At this point the child is in the rapprochement subphase. An attachment bond is in place, the mother and child interact in such a way that the child experiences him/herself mirrored and marked, a true self is in place, self and other are demarcated, and object constancy is established.

Here we have the analytic precursors of different types of attachment experiences (Ainsworth et al., 1978) dually determined by the infant's constitution and the mother's inclination noted in today's parlance as secure and insecure attachment: avoidant, resistant, and disorganized. Noted here as well is how these are transmitted from one generation to the next (Slade, 1999, Fonagy et al., 1993).

Mahler's focus was on the vicissitudes of this early relationship, the pinnacle being the establishment of self and object constancy, at which point children have developed a solid sense of self and other. It is this that allows the child to go out and meet the world on a secure footing, to relate, to test reality, to move from psychic reality to pretend mode, to learn to play, symbolize, think, and develop a healthy superego, all of the accomplishments required to create a lie.

Once the bond has been established the child can then proceed to develop a clearly demarcated internalized sense of self and other. Without this there can be no lying as lying can only take place in the presence of another whether this other is external or internal. One needs another to lie. Recall the definition of lying as deceitfulness or intent to mislead. Another is both implied and essential.

It is in the rapprochement subphase that a beginning internal demarcated sense of self and other, the basic intrapsychic requirement for lying, is established. As the child oscillates between autonomy and connectedness, between independence and dependency the requisite cognitive and emotional development occurs.

And it is at this point that the development of our first grade algebra whiz, Alex, faltered. She came to see me, as she was both unable to leave her mother's side and unable to allow herself to depend on anyone for anything. She was adequately although insecurely attached and had difficulty separating herself out from another. Her parents made almost no demands on her, giving in to her slightest whim and praising her for the most minor accomplishment. This seems to have left her with a false sense of self, with no realistic idea of who she was or of what she was capable. It is in this context that she claims she is able to do advanced math. Possibly this is a wish that is experienced as a truth and a reflection of her inauthentic self. This needs to be differentiated from lying.

Representational Object Constancy

Tyson (1996), integrating cognitive and psychoanalytic milestones elucidates three stages of object constancy. The first stage is attained when the infant is able to maintain a constant investment in the object irrespective of drive gratification. This correlates with social referencing: the infant coping by referencing the mother's face for affective signals and using this as a means of self-regulation. There is an attachment to the human face and the ability to utilize it for its signaling function. Here we note Spitz's first and second psychic organizers, the recognition of the gestalt of the human face and then of the mother's face as special. This seems to be where Alex has landed.

Tyson's second stage is representational object constancy, a stage Alex has not quite attained. This correlates with developments occurring at about eighteen months: Mahler's rapprochement subphase, evocative mental representation, the development of speech, and symbolic function. Representations, characterized by sensory-motor thinking, tend to be concrete and highly influenced by emotionally charged events. However, they remain stable and available. Wishes and demands ordered and categorized can now be differentiated from self-interest. Organizing, categorizing, and labeling inner and outer worlds bring the potential for mastery. They also bring the toddler face to face with the differences between his wishes and his mother's expectations noted behaviorally in the emergence of ambi-tendency as the child vacillates between expressing his wishes and countering them. Conflict emerges with fantasies of consequences should mother's demands not be met. This promotes and requires compromise and conflict resolution. The child now has not only the intrapsychic requirements but also the motivation to lie. And here we note Celia's insistence on no 'poopy' as well as Alex's faltering development.

The third stage of object constancy is Mahler's libidinal object constancy in which the representation of the object has become an inner source of sustenance, comfort, and love (Mahler and Furer, 1968, p.222). A very advanced stage of development has been attained.

We have established a secure attachment, a true self, a demarcation of self and object with some degree of constancy, Mahler's rapprochement subphase and Tyson's representational object constancy. Next, we turn to the development of reflective function or mentalization. Although I am listing these attainments in what might seem to be a developmental line, I need to emphasize that they are not necessarily linear developments and that they interact with and promote the development of each other.

Reflective Functioning
Reflective functioning is the capacity to reflect on mental states and attribute intention to thoughts, feelings, and acts both within oneself and in others. It allows for a move out of the psychic equivalence mode of functioning in which psychic reality and physical reality are equivalent (Fonagy and Target, 1996; Target and Fonagy, 1996). Alex's sense of omnipotence, that she can do algebra, whatever that means to her, is experienced as her reality not

to be confronted or contradicted. For her, inner and outer realities are one and the same. Inner experience reflects external reality and others' experiences are considered identical with her own.

By reflecting on the child's mind and offering another mind for the child to explore, the parent supplies a road to reflective functioning. The child's sense of self as a separate individual with a mind of its own as well as a consideration of mental states within oneself and others is fostered. Fonagy considers this the birth of the psychological self as "my caregiver thinks of me as a thinking person and therefore I exist as a thinker." Awareness of mental states leads to finding meaning in one's own and others' behavior. To lie, one must have abandoned total reliance on psychic equivalence, be aware of one's wishes as wishes and be aware of the other as having a mind of his or her own which may not be consonant with one's own wishes. Alex had not completed this step. She was not always aware that her wishes were wishes and that others might have a different view of the situation. She wished it and therefore it must be so. She was quite upset when this did not prove to be the case as when she wished for mother's protective presence and mother did not magically appear.

As the child begins to distinguish thoughts and wishes from external reality, she turns to the use of the pretend mode (Target and Fonagy, 1996). In this mode ideas are represented but their correspondence with reality is not examined or questioned. Whereas in psychic reality the child's thoughts and feelings are experienced as truth, in the pretend mode the child is able to play out all manner of feelings and scenarios as long as they are kept separated out from reality. A clear distinction between play/pretend and reality must be maintained. Any attempt to connect the two, for example, the fighting in the doll house to the fighting at home, is denied vehemently, ignored, or leads to a shutting down and/or withdrawal.

The pretend mode, separated out from reality, allows for an opportunity to play out different schema, try on different roles, and experience how it feels. Different possibilities, different ways of handling or understanding situations can be explored. The child running down the beach claiming to be Superman is pretending. It is important to separate this out from lying. He is not attempting to mislead or deceive. He is trying on a role figuring out what it might feel like to have superpowers. In pretense there is a dual process going on. While the child is in the experience of being Superman, he does not question the reality of it, yet it is also not his sole truth.

Play is essential in linking inner and outer reality so that they no longer need to be either equated or split off. Integration of the two modes of functioning, psychic reality and pretense, takes place within the playful interaction between parent and child. It is the caretaker's reflecting on and playing with the child's experience that brings this about.

One of the important functions of the parent in this play is maintaining affect at a comfortable level so that the child can allow the play to proceed. This, of course, is comparable to what goes on in child analysis. It demands a high level of attunement and sensitivity to the child's limits. It also requires that the parents contain their own anxiety. This was a problem for Alex as her father withdrew when anxiety was touched upon and her mother became frantic. She anticipated the same response from her analyst. Her development faltered, as her parents were unable to play with her ideas and feelings without being overwhelmed with anxiety, hers and theirs. Opportunity to make a link with reality yielding a sense of existence outside of the child's mind was lost as they were unable to play with reality to produce a pretend yet real mental experience.

Enhanced Cognitive and Emotional Development
Reflective functioning is a significant turning point in cognitive and emotional development. It enables the child to see people's actions as meaningful and therefore predictable thereby diminishing dependency on others and enhancing individuation. It allows distinction between inner and outer truths, opens communication, and enhances intersubjectivity. As the capacity to test ideas against reality develops, the impact of ideas and feelings is moderated. Affect is less overwhelming and fears can now be played with and made safer.

After an extensive period of analysis, Alex was able to begin to ask for my help, turn to me, and depend on me sometimes and in some ways. She was able to see that anxiety did not always become overwhelming. This gave me an opportunity to reflect on and play with her ideas and feelings thereby promoting even greater enhancement of affect containment. Gradually she became able to see that there were rules with which to abide that made life with others less chaotic, more even, and predictable. And that her teacher was not particularly targeting her and that sometimes the other girls just wanted to do something else as they had wishes of their own that they wanted to play out. And then she began to be able to utilize imaginative play to gain some insight into other people and new situations.

She no longer claimed to be able to do advanced math as she had a more realistic view of herself and of her capabilities. She no longer claimed extraordinary abilities as she became more reflective and came to terms with wishes and reality. But as this is still a work in progress, evidence of earlier modes of operation are noted as she claims to have a dog, which is not permitted in her home, and in the making of an extensive list of all of her many friends. These are clearly wishes not clearly differentiated from fantasy or reality. Reflective function promoting enhanced reality testing differentiating fantasy from reality is a necessary attainment for lying. In order to lie, one must have a belief that one has a mind that can conjure up independent ideas that are different from those of another and can influence the other. Alex was just beginning to establish this.

The Capacity to Play

For the child analyst at work, the word 'play' conjures up images of therapy with Oedipal age children. This is pretend play at its best as the child is capable of suspending disbelief and engaging in pretense, has some understanding of how others think, has the verbal ability to convey thoughts, and is not hampered by latency superego restrictions prohibiting free fantasy expression.

However, play begins long before the oedipal phase. It begins with the child exploring his body (Freud, A., 1965), within what Winnicott (1953) refers to as the transitional space. This is the space between child and mother within which the child plays and learns. In this space inner and outer are united and out of this space ego boundaries gradually differentiate. It is here that unconscious wishes meet reality and conflict emerges. Play leads to resolution by the creation of a world of illusion meeting the demands of the desires and the prohibitions they confront. Play rearranges the world to suit.

So play is a means of coming to terms with reality—the reality of separateness and dependency on the nurturing adult whose adaptation to the child's needs and wishes is not perfect. As the illusion that the mother is part of the baby and under omnipotent control can no longer be sustained, the child plays with reality and develops a transitional object. In this intermediate area of illusion, the me-not me object supplies the illusion of omnipotent control. Later in the child's life, fantasy play replaces the transitional object offering its own way of coming to terms with reality and with those problems that reality presents.

There is a developmental trajectory from play on the body to play in the transitional space, to the use of the transitional object to the utilization of fantasy. The advent of fantasy allows the child to imagine other roles, other minds, and other solutions, all of which advance development and help prepare for the future. Mastery is promoted, communication enhanced, reality is dealt with and a greater understanding of the world, the mind, the self, and the other is attained. New ideas are tested and a verbal narrative develops.

But it is the all-important oedipal reorganization that determines and allows for a flourishing of imaginative, symbolic play. The child can now engage in conversation with different aspects of self and of others, integrate the dichotomous sense of gender, learn to control and tolerate intimacy, and develop affect tolerance. Multiple story lines are brought together as play portrays the wish for connection and the wish for autonomy, the wish for power and the fear of retaliation, and the multiple fantasies of body and gender. A narrative is formed.

Imaginative drama flourishes allowing us to gain insight into the child's inner world. Symbolic representation of impulse, affect, and fantasy now substitute for immediate gratification. Mastery is experienced as play, allows the child to titrate fantasy and reality, modify wishes, and better tolerate limitation of reality and capabilities. When conflict is evoked, consequences and solutions can now be considered in multiple ways. The child becomes the director of his different scenarios. He is no longer a passive victim. This, in itself, often serves as an important substitute for the realization of wishes. Verbalization, displacement, and mastery are key elements in the effectiveness of play. And then play, as we know it in the oedipal child, diminishes in importance as latency brings with it greater symbolic capacities and efforts now turn toward a different kind of mastery.

Of course, we retain our capacity to play. We use it throughout the lifespan. It becomes an important component of parental activity (Mahon, 1993) and it is an important component of psychoanalysis (Winnicott, 1971). A highly developed use of play is necessary for analytic free association in which there is a suspension of reality requiring the ability to pretend, suspend judgment, and imagine. And all of this takes place in the transitional space between analysand and analyst in which the analysand can meet and use the analyst. And this brings us to Ms. A, the analysand, who plays in the analytic space but avoids certain topics and affects preferring to hold on to an important false idea rather than explore and discover some unwanted truth. There is a limit to what we will play and what we will play with. This is true for all of us.

One More Developmental Requirement

So in addition to the seven developmental attainments I have delineated, I would add an eighth—the oedipal organization as an ultimate requirement for full-fledged lying. It is only then that the child can pull together fantasy, reality, conflict, and compromise, develop a narrative, know the difference between reality and pretense, feel the pressure of the prohibiting superego, and attempt to mislead or deceive the other.

In the midst of pulling together my thoughts on this topic, I received a call from our son informing us that his wife had delivered a healthy little girl. We went to meet the new arrival who was indeed bright and beautiful. She nursed, slept, cried, molded to her mother's body, opened her eyes, checked out the surroundings, looked away, and fell asleep. It was too early for her to be attached or to have acquired any of the milestones I had been so busily delineating. She certainly was not up to lying.

Her two-year-old sister, however, was another interesting story. She was securely attached with a fairly clearly demarcated authentic sense of self and other. All this she clearly expressed in her effusive verbosity. She had a great deal to say on any number of topics. One of her favorite activities was having someone read to her—an ideal activity for a grandmother. I had come prepared with what I thought was a wonderful book of poems. They were simple, short, and fun, with beautiful pictures. We were really into it until I came upon the poem "Jam on Toast" that reads, "Why is strawberry jam so red? Why is toast so brown? Why when I drop it on the floor, Is it always jam side down?"

She suddenly became very sad, closed the book, and left the room. Her father explained that there are other books that she will not read. They make her too sad or frightened. What was going on here? An overwhelming emotion led to a loss of reflective functioning in this particular arena. The idea of something falling down felt too real and was too affect-laden. She could neither maintain it in the realm of fantasy nor could she play with it. Her vivid imagination that allowed her to imagine all sorts of scenarios, problems, and solutions suddenly led her into dangerous waters. It just felt too real and too scary. She abandoned the project. She had established many of the prerequisites—the attachment, distinct sense of self and other, reflective functioning, rapprochement subphase, Tyson's second stage of object constancy, pretense—the ability to creatively imagine many stories, even manipulate reality by tricking her father and laughing when she was successful in this endeavor, thereby demonstrating intent to mislead. She was just coming into her own in the ability to lie or be deceitful.

Back to the Beginning

Celia at two and a half said, no poopy. Several months later she put on a special dress and announced that she was a princess. Her mommy was the queen. I made the mistake of assuming therefore that her daddy was the king. She quickly corrected me, telling me that daddy was the prince and that grandpa would be the king. This was strikingly consonant with Little Hans' imaginings. Oedipal fantasies and an oedipal organization had been established and she was showing greater evidence of intent to mislead.

And several months later still, she put on a cape and, like Dan, ran around pretending to be Superman. If asked if she was really Superman, really flying, she would be surprised by the question and would claim that she was merely pretending. She, like Dan, knew the truth of her non-Superman self. She was playing that she could fly and accomplish feats of omnipotence, no doubt to relieve the tension of a sense of powerlessness not to deceive or mislead others. Her earlier sense of being the princess to her daddy's prince was more clearly or totally in the realm of pretense cut off from psychic reality. Integration of psychic reality and pretense was more fully accomplished in the Superman play.

In exploring Alex's claim of knowing algebra, we can appreciate her narcissistic vulnerability, the possibility of an inauthentic self, even her intent to mislead. But who is the target? Is it herself or is it the other? Is it justified to label this as lying? The adolescent denying drug use seems to be more clearly lying but how about the analysand who assiduously avoids certain topics and affects? Would we consider this lying? And how about Kakutani's list of the plethora of deception she notes in Wolff's characters and in the use of deception in the very act of fiction writing itself? The topic is clearly a complex one. It is not simple or as black and white as is so often assumed and I have certainly not clarified or even touched on all of the vicissitudes of this fascinating topic of lying. My effort has been merely to clarify some of the necessary developmental prerequisites.

References

Ainsworth, M.D.S., Blehar, M.C., Waters, E., and Wall, S. (1978). *Patterns of Attachment: A Psychological Study of the Strange Situation*. Hillsdale, NJ: Lawrence Erlbaum.

Blum, H.P. (2007). Little Hans: A centennial reconsideration. *Journal of the American Psychoanalytic Association* 55: 749–765.

Emde, R.N. (1980). Toward a psychoanalytic theory of affect: part 1, the organizational model and its propositions. In: *The Course of Life: Infancy and Early Childhood*, ed. S.I. Greenspan and G. H. Pollock, pp. 63–83. Adelphi, MD: National Institute of Mental Health.

Fonagy, P. (2001). *Attachment Theory and Psychoanalysis*. New York: Other Press

Fonagy, P., Steele, H., Moran, G., Steele, M., and Higgitt, A. (1993). Measuring the ghost in the nursery: an empirical study of the relation between parents, mental representations of childhood experiences and their infants' security of attachment. *Journal of the American Psychoanalytic Association* 441: 957–989.

Fonagy, P. and Target, M. (1996). Playing with reality1: theory of mind and the normal development of psychic reality. *International Journal of Psychoanalysis* 77: 217–233.

Fonagy, P., Target, M., Gergely, G., Allen, J. and Bateman, A. (2003). The developmental roots of borderline personality disorder in early attachment relationships: a theory and some evidence. *Psychoanalytic Inquiry* 23: 412–459.

Fraiberg, S. (1987). *Selected Writings of Selma Fraiberg*. Columbus, OH: Ohio State University Press.

Freud, A. (1941–1945). Reports on the Hampstead nurseries. In: *The Writings of Anna Freud*. New York: International Universities Press, 1974.

Freud, A. (1965). *Normality and Pathology in Childhood*. New York: International Universities Press.

Freud, A. and Burlingham, D. (1944). *Infants Without Families*. New York: International Universities Press.

Freud, S. (1909). Analysis of a phobia in a five-year-old boy. *Standard Edition* 10: 5–147.

Freud, S. (1913). Two lies told by children. *Standard Edition* 12.

Gergely, G. and Watson, J (1996). The social biofeedback theory of parental affect mirroring: the development of emotional, self-awareness and self-control in infancy. *International Journal of Psychoanalysis* 77: 1181–1212.

Greenacre, P. (1958). The relation of the impostor to the artist. In: *Emotional Growth, Vol 2*. New York: International Universities Press, 1971

Halpert, E. (2000). On lying and the lie of the toddler. *Psychoanalytic Quarterly* 69: 659–675.

Kakutani, M. (2008). 'Review of *Our Story Begins*, by Tobias Wolff,' Book Review Section, New York Times, March 28.

Kohut, H. (1971). *The Analysis of the Self*. New York: International Universities Press.

Lyons-Ruth, K. (2006). The interface between attachment and intersubjectivity: Perspective from the longitudinal study of disorganized attachment. *Psychoanalytic Inquiry* 26: 595–615.

Mahler, M., Pine, F., and Bergman, A. (1975). *The Psychological Birth of the Human Infant: Symbiosis and Individuation*. New York: Basic Books.

Mahon, E. (1993). Play, parenthood, and creativity. In: *The Many Meanings of Play*, ed. A. Solnit, D. Cohen, and P. Neubauer. New Haven, CT: Yale University Press, 1993.

Owen, G. (2007). Jam on toast. In: *Here's a Little Poem*, eds. J. Yolen and A. Peters, p. 21. Cambridge, MA: Candlewick Press.

Pine, F. (2004). Mahler's concepts of "symbiosis" and separation-individuation revisited, reevaluated, refined. *Journal of the American Psychoanalytic Association* 52: 511–533.

Schore, A. (1994). *Affect Regulation and the Origins of the Self*. Hillsdale, NJ: The Analytic Press.

Schore, A. (1997). A century after Freud's project: is a rapprochement between psychoanalysis and neurobiology at hand? *Journal of the American Psychoanalytic Association* 45: 807–840.

Schore, A. (2002). Advances in neuro-psychoanalysis, attachment theory and trauma research: implications for self psychology. *Psychoanalytic Inquiry* 22: 433–484.

Slade, A. (1999). Representation, symbolization, and affect regulation in the concomitant treatment of a mother and child: attachment theory and child psychotherapy. *Psychoanalytic Inquiry* 19: 797–830.

Spitz, R. (1965). *The First Year of Life*. New York: International Universities Press.

Stern, D. (1985). *The Interpersonal World of the Infant*. New York: Basic Books.

Target, M. and Fonagy, P. (1996). Playing with reality: II. the development of psychic reality from a theoretical perspective. *International Journal of Psychoanalysis*.

Tyson, P. (1996). Object relations, affect management and psychic structure formation: the concept of object constancy. *Psychoanalytic Study of the Child* 51: 172–189.

Weinshel, E.M. (1979). Some observations on not telling the truth. *Journal of the American Psychoanalytic Association* 27: 503–531.

Wilkinson, S. and Hough, G. (1996). Lies as narrative truth in abused adopted adolescents. *Psychoanalytic Study of the Child* 51: 580–596.

Winnicott, D.W. (1953). Transitional objects and transitional phenomena. *International Journal of Psychoanalysis* 34: 89–97

Winnicott, D.W. (1965). *The Maturational Processes and the Facilitating Environment*. London: Hogarth.

Winnicott, D.W. (1971). *Playing and Reality*. London: Tavistock.

~

CHAPTER THREE

Developmental Aspects of Lying

Gail A. Edelsohn, M.D., M.S.P.H.

Dr. Ruth Fischer takes a developmental perspective on the topic of lying and discusses the intrapsychic capabilities required to lie. She suggests the following eight prerequisites for the emergence and consolidation of the capacity to lie:

1. having obtained an attachment bond
2. having developed a sense of self from others
3. negotiation of rapprochement subphase and achievement of object constancy
4. demonstrating reflective function
5. having achieved a certain level of cognitive development
6. having developed a distinction of reality from fantasy
7. having the ability to play
8. reaching a stage of an oedipal organization.

I would like to expand on these developmental requirements by reviewing some normal developmental research on lying, maintaining a lie, and disclosure.

Preschoolers

By the fourth birthday, most children will experiment with lying to avoid punishment and they will lie indiscriminately whenever punishment seems to be a possibility. Parents frequently are left to say but I saw you hit your sister or climb up on the counter to their three- to five-year-olds. We know that young children like to make up stories and tell tall tales. They enjoy having stories told to them and they enjoy making up their own stories. Think of long-standing popular and classic children's books—*Where the Wild Things Are*, think as well about books where the lead character has an adventure, gets in trouble but is still loved, such as the series of *Curious George* books. Young children may blur the distinction between reality and fantasy. Fantasy play at this age is typical of normal development and often encouraged.

Dr. Fischer writes, "Lying is defined as deceitfulness, the intentional use of lies, untruthfulness, intent to mislead or be fraudulent, not telling the whole truth." Let us examine another definition that suggests an appreciation of theory of mind is a critical aspect in lying. Lee's (2000) definition of lying elaborates and extends Dr. Fischer's intentional quality of lying to the act by which one not only deliberately states an untruth but also does so with the intention to put false convictions into the mind of the lie's recipient.

To put is simply, lying is a developmental skill. Talwar, Gordon, and Lee (2007) explain the steps involved in lying that reflect children's understanding of a theory of mind. To lie a child must recognize the truth, think of an alternative reality, be able to convince someone else of their constructed false statements, be able to appreciate their own and the recipient's mental state, and whether the recipient is ignorant about the true situation that the lie teller has knowledge of. The lie teller must be able to make statements that will not make the recipient suspicious, and demonstrate verbal and nonverbal behaviors that support the lie. The application of the theory of mind with regards to lying, harkens back to one of the intrapsychic requirements for lying having a sense of self and other, but I propose it goes further to encompass a sense of what the other is thinking and so bears some similarity to another requirement noted by Dr. Fischer, reflective functioning. By studying lie telling in children, according to Talwar, Gordon, and Lee (2007) we can begin to understand how children use their theory of mind in everyday life.

Preschool Research

A limited number of studies use a modified temptation resistance paradigm (Chandler, Fritz, and Hala, 1989; Lewis, Stanger, and Sullivan; 1989: Polak and Harris, 1999; Talwar and Lee, 2002; Talwar, Lee, Bala, and Lindsay, 2002). Children are given the chance to commit a transgression, looking at a forbidden object (such as a toy), and then lie spontaneously about it. Researchers refer to this as the "Peeking Game." The ability to lie can be detected in children as young as three and rapidly develops with age. Some preschoolers can conceal their lies, but are not very skilled. Children have to not only tell a believable lie, they have to maintain consistency between the lie and subsequent statements. This ability to maintain consistency is referred to as 'semantic leakage control' (Talwar and Lee, 2002). Only a couple of studies have explored this issue. Both find that children between three and five are not capable of semantic leakage control. When they are asked to identify a toy after they say they have not peeked at it, they blurt out the answer and do not feign ignorance. So most three- to five-year-olds implicate themselves as having lied. There is a developmental trend with about 50 percent of six- to seven-year-olds (who indeed have peeked) feigning ignorance of the toy's identity and so concealing their lie.

Researchers (Polak and Harris, 1999 and Talwar and Lee, 2002) make the case that a sophisticated theory of mind understanding is needed to maintain semantic leakage control. What does this mean? Faking ignorance to follow up questions requires children to represent second order states. In the temptation resistance situation, children can go with the experimenter's perspective and first assume that the experimenter thinks they have no knowledge of the answer because they said they did not peek (which is a false belief). Children then need to reason about what the experimenter expects them to know or not know (a second order belief). After lying about not looking at the forbidden object, when asked about the identity of the toy, children would have to work through—well the experimenter believes that I do not know the identity of the forbidden object—in order to fake ignorance. The task for the child is to represent a belief about someone else's belief to be able to maintain the consistency between the lie " I didn't look" and the subsequent statements.

Elementary School Years

The reasons for lying become more complex when a child reaches elementary school. The top reason is still to avoid punishment, but lying can serve other functions—to increase a child's sense of control and power, to manipulate friends with teasing, to bolster status by bragging, and by learning he or she can pull one over on his/her parents. However, in elementary school, children may lie to their peers as a coping mechanism, when they are frustrated or as a way to get attention. Any sudden increase in lying is a warning signal—something is troubling the youngster. The good news is in longitudinal studies, a majority of six-year-olds who frequently lie have it socialized out of them by age seven. If lying has become a successful way of coping in difficult social situations, then a child will continue with lying.

What do we know from normal developmental studies about lying? Around age six, research has shown that second order mental state understanding begins to emerge and continues to develop into adolescence. Talwar and Gordon (2007) studied children between six and eleven (n = 116) to specifically examine their semantic leakage control ability and its connection to second order thought belief understanding. The experiment used a trivia game, with questions and four possible answers on one side of the card. On the back of the card was the correct answer written in a different color ink and an unrelated picture. Children received a token for each correct answer. They could win a prize after earning three tokens. After two questions, the experimenter said she had to leave the room for a minute. The children's behavior was recorded by a hidden camera. When she returned, she asked, did you peek? Then she asked the final trivia question. If they gave the correct answer, she asked how had they arrived at it. To this, the children gave three responses: a plausible explanation, a claim that they simply guessed, or that they just did not know. Children who did not peek, would be expected to guess the correct answer 25 percent of the time. All children received the third token and all children got a prize.

The experimenter told the children the game was over, but she had two questions before they left. These are entrapment questions to see if they would feign ignorance to conceal their peeking. What is the color of the writing on the back of the card? What animal is shown on the back of the card? If children who peeked at the answer lied about peeking and were poor at semantic leakage control, they would be more likely to give the correct answer. But if they were skilled at lying, their response should be similar to those who did not peek. There was a control condition where the children were told they were allowed to peek at the answer in order to rule out the possibility that children might forget or not notice the color of the writing or the animal picture on the back of the card. In addition, nonverbal expressive behavior was recorded and coded. The children were also given a theory of mind task that involved watching a video story and being asked targeted questions.

So what are the results for elementary school aged students? Contrary to the previous preschool studies, where the majority of children peeked, only half of the school age children peeked. Younger children were more likely to peek than older children, consistent with normative development and increasing inhibitory control. Ninety-three percent of children who peeked at the answer denied doing so. So the tendency to lie about transgressions continued beyond preschool into elementary school.

The third hypothesis was that older children who denied transgression would demonstrate semantic leakage control. Overall, lie tellers answered the entrapment questions correctly more often than nonliars. However, incorrect answers increased with age. Younger lie tellers were more likely to answer the entrapment questions correctly than were third and fifth grade lie tellers. As all the control children answered the follow up questions correctly, it is highly likely that the lie tellers deliberately answered at least one entrapment question incorrectly to cover their lie

The last major question regarding theory of mind revealed that children's tendency to feign ignorance was significantly related to their second order belief understanding as predicted by the theory of mind task. Children who had lower second order belief understanding were less likely to fake ignorance when answering the entrapment questions.

Children's second order belief understanding was not related to their non-verbal expression. Semantic leakage control increased with age but also with increased cognitive sophistication as reflected by second order belief understanding. Is this good news or not? This study points to an association between skillful deception and enhanced understanding of theory of mind. Although lies are an outward expression of dishonesty, which is not congruent with prosocial values, it has been said that the ability to lie is a sign of intellect.

Another Experiment with Implications for Clinical Work and Parental Advice

In different studies, researchers read the child a moral tale before asking about peeking (Bronson, 2008). One story is The Boy Who Cried Wolf—the one that ends with both the boy and the sheep eaten due to many repeated lies. The other is the George Washington and the Cherry Tree story. The story ends with George's father saying—"George, I'm glad that you cut down the tree after all. Hearing you tell the truth instead of a lie is better than if I had a thousand cherry trees."

Which story cuts down on lying more? Please give a show of hands—the boy who cried wolf (vote) or George Washington and the cherry tree ? Most of the symposium attendees voted for The Boy Who Cried Wolf as having more impact on reducing lying. The Boy Who Cried Wolf story actually made things a little worse. The George Washington and The Cherry Tree story reduced lying by 43 percent in children compared to the control situation who were not read a short story before being questioned about peeking. The shepherd boy gets death as a punishment. Increasing punishment for lying, only makes children more cognizant of the potential personal cost. It does not teach children how lying impacts others. In some studies, children who are always under the threat of punishment do not lie less. They learn how to become more adept at lying and how to avoid being caught.

The process of socialization is what teaches children not to lie, and parents need to teach the value of being honest as much as that lies are bad. Talwar from McGill has expressed the concern that indirectly parents teach children to lie by engaging in white lies and encouraging white lies. Her examples—on the phone to telemarketer—"I'm just a guest here." "They see us boast and lie to smooth social relationships" (Bronson, 2008).

What message do parents teach to children when you get a gift you don't like? The not-so-great gift experiment. Children play a game to win a prize, but the prize is . . . a bar of soap. The researcher gives them a moment to compose themselves, then asks—how they like it. A quarter of preschoolers can lie that they like it. By elementary school—half can lie. Telling the lie makes them uncomfortable, especially when asked to give a reason why they like the bar of soap. However, the parents are usually pleased the child came up with a white lie and proud they are polite. Parents don't see that white lies are still lies.

With the help of diaries, adults admit to lying about once every five social interactions, which averages out to once a day. Most of these are white lies. Children hear a lot of white lies and are encouraged to tell them. They get comfortable with being insincere. The lesson they learn is that honesty causes conflict and dishonesty is a way to avoid it. Children don't confuse the white lie situation with lying to cover transgressions, they do transfer the emotional groundwork from one circumstance to the other. This makes it psychologically easier to lie to a parent. A child buys something with his own allowance that the parent feels is wasteful. Where did you get these . . . cartoon stickers? I told you not to waste your allowance on this type of trash. The child may feel this is a white lie scenario and he can make the father feel better by telling him his friend gave him the stickers.

Adolescence and Lying

Mahler wrote about separation individuation. Separation and the push for independence are again confronted in adolescence. Autonomy in adolescence is often tied to the need to protect one's privacy and an unwillingness to disclose personal information to parents. Reflect on some version of these conversations with your own adolescent offspring.

Parent: "Where are you going?"

Adolescent: "Just out."

Parent: "With whom?"

Adolescent: "Oh I don't know exactly who will show up."

Parent: "Well will you be with . . . (name the friend(s) you most disapprove of).

Parent: "Will John be driving?" (you know the one that drinks and drives)

Darling and colleagues (2000) have studied what happens when adolescents and parents disagree about what are the legitimate domains of parental control. Direct communication about the disagreement is only one choice. Adolescents may choose to avoid confrontation or disclose only some of the details parents want to know, or they may choose to lie about their beliefs, behaviors, or plans. As children become adolescents, they have improved perspective taking and may try to calculate the parents' reaction if they tell the whole truth.

A study done by Darling et al. (2000), that was carried out while she was at Penn State, looked at adolescent agreement with parents, decisions on what to do in cases of disagreement, and their reasons for disclosing or not disclosing. She found adolescents most likely to agree with parents when they think a parent has a right to set rules about the issue and when they consider the issue unimportant. In cases of disagreement when they believe a parent has a right to set rules about the issue, they are more likely to avoid the issue or leave out important information. When they believe parents DO NOT have the right to set rules about the issue they are more likely to either tell them or lie. Adolescents are most likely to disclose and least likely to lie when the issue is important to them. They are more likely to lie when they think the issue is unimportant.

Why do adolescents decide to disclose their disagreement with parents? Older adolescents are more likely to tell because they think they should. Younger adolescents are more likely to tell because they hope the parents will change their mind. Why do adolescents choose nondisclosure? When adolescents believe the parents have a right to set rules about the issue they disagree with, they choose not to disclose for emotional reasons, such as embarrassment or concern the parent will worry. When adolescents do not think parents have a legitimate right to set rules they are more likely to be motivated by fear of consequences or belief that the issue is none of their parents' business.

Darling also mailed surveys to the parents of teens interviewed. Parents who were permissive really don't learn more about their children's lives. Parents who don't set rules have kids that go wild. Youth take the lack of rules to mean that parents don't care. Parents worry too many rules will push adolescents into rebellion. Most parents with lots of rules don't really enforce them. Parents who had a few key rules in certain areas, explained why they had them and expected the child to obey. The same parents supported autonomy in other areas and allowed them to make decisions. The teens of these parents lied the least.

To many lying is the opposite of honesty and agreeing is the opposite of arguing. Adolescents see arguing as the opposite of lying. How does this work? In families where there was less deception, there was a higher ratio of arguing and complaining. With arguments, the teens were honest. Certain types of fighting were ultimately signs of respect, not of disrespect. A separate study by Holmes (Bronson, 2008) looks at mothers and teens and how they perceived arguments. Forty-six percent of mothers rated arguments as destructive to their relationships with their teens. They saw it as stressful, chaotic, and disrespectful. The more often they fought, the more the moms saw it as harmful. But only 23 percent of teens saw it is harmful. They felt it strengthened their relationships with their mothers. Adolescents saw fighting as seeing their parents differently and hearing their mothers' point of view be articulated. In the Holmes study, the teens did not rate fighting as harmful or destructive even if they fought often or had big fights; however, no one had an extreme amount of conflict. What really mattered was how the arguments got resolved.

Concluding Remarks

Honesty and lying are learned in the home. I believe Dr. Fischer's intrapsychic developmental requirements are complemented by the research on normal development of children's ability to lie, their social cognition, the importance of relationships especially to parents, and motivation for telling lies, disclosure and nondisclosure.

References

Bronson, P. (2008). Learning to Lie. Available at www.nymag.com/news/features/43893.

Chandler, M., Fritz, A.S., and Hala, S. (1989). Small-scale deceit: deception as a marker of two-, three-, and four-year olds' early theories of mind. *Child Development* 60: 1263–1277.

Darling, N., Hames, K., and Cumsille, P. (2000). "Parents and adolescents disagree: disclosure strategies and motivations," presented at the Society for Research in Adolescence 2000 Biennial meetings, The Pennsylvania State University: University Park, Pennsylvania.

Lee, K. (2000). Lying as doing deceptive things with words. A speech act theoretical perspective. In: J.W. Astington, ed., *Minds in the Making: Essays in Honour of David R. Olson* (pp. 177–196). Oxford: Blackwell.

Lewis, M., Stranger, C., and Sullivan, M.W. (1989). Deception in 3-year-olds. *Developmental Psychology* 25: 439–443.

Polak, A. and Harris, P.L. (1999). Deception in young children following noncompliance. *Developmental Psychology* 35: 561–568.

Talwar, V., Gordon, H.M., and Lee, K. (2007). Lying in the elementary school years: verbal deception and its relation to second-order belief understanding. *Developmental Psychology* 43(3): 804–810.

Talwar, V. and Lee, K. (2002). Development of lying to conceal a transgression: children's control of expressive behavior during verbal deception. *International Journal of Behavioral Development* 26: 436–444.

Talwar, V., Lee, K., Bala, N., and Lindsay, T.C.I. (2002). Children's conception knowledge of lie-telling and its relation to their actual behaviors: implications for court competence examination. *Law and Human Behavior* 26: 395–415.

CHAPTER FOUR

~

Authentication, Imposture, and Malicious Deception

Lucy LaFarge, M.D.

Early in my career, a woman who was soon to begin analysis tried to explain to me the complexities of her difficult family. Relationships were strained between the parents and among the children; alliances were unstable; and even the most durable ties could not be relied upon; intense quarrels would break out and new lines would be drawn. Trying to make sense of the complicated history that she presented, I asked what the quarrels were about. My patient paused for a moment to reflect, then replied, "*In my family we argue about reality.*"

What did my patient mean? As analysts, we are attentive to family dramas and the ways they come alive between patient and analyst in the analytic process. Likely, with the question I asked, I was trying not only to learn my patient's history but also, tentatively, to place myself within the story of her family, to try on one or another of the many roles in which I might be cast in the analysis that would follow. Would I be the mother who, in this early version of the patient's story, turned away from her in early childhood? The father who rescued her only to drop her later on in favor of her sister?

Instead, my patient drew my attention to a second story that stood in the background of her family drama: *Who decided* what the mother and father were like and what they had done? Who determined who the patient was? Did the story change abruptly from moment to moment? And between us, how would the truth of the patient's experience be determined? Would one of us make it up? Discover it? Would we argue about it? And what was at stake if we did? Would she simply be whoever we said she was? How solid was anything after all? Perhaps even her history might be entirely different than she thought!

Over the years since then I have come to see that this woman was one of many patients for whom the second story—the story of how reality is constructed and by whom—is more important than the first. For these patients, who suffer from narcissistic pathology of one kind or another, fantasies about the way reality and the self are constructed and change are central to mental life. In analysis, these fantasies are sometimes conscious and make up part of the patient's spoken associations. More often they surface in the form of subtle enactments that may come to dominate transference and counter-transference.

Although fantasies about reality construction are highly varied and assume unique shapes for every individual, in their fundamental form these fantasies depict an object relationship, a parent and child, engaged together in imagining the child's experience. Who is the parent that imagines the child and how does she go about imagining? Is he able to imagine well? Is she able to imagine only by thinking and not by feeling? Are certain areas of the parent's responsiveness felt by the child to be dulled or closed off? And how is the child's own experience affected by the parent's imagining of it? In a series of papers (LaFarge, 2004, 2006, 2008) I have explored some of the forms that may be taken by these fantasies, which I have called *fantasies of the imaginer and the imagined,* as well as the clinical usefulness of the analyst's attention to them, particularly in the treatment of narcissistic patients.

Fantasies of imaginer and imagined are present in everyone, but they often remain quite silent, an unobserved background to other more colorful stories. They draw upon historical experience, and are also importantly shaped by wishful and defensive fantasy. For narcissistic patients, fantasies of the imaginer and the imagined are prominent; and they tend to be highly distorted; often they are split. The imagining parent may be seen alternately as ideally understanding and as malignantly annihilating; and the effect of the parent's imagining may be felt to be magically transformative, remaking the child's entire self, by loving attention into a new and ideal version, or by inattention or rejection, into a worthless and rageful shell. As these fantasies emerge in analysis, the patient may remain stably in the role of the imagined child, with the analyst cast in the role of the imagining parent, or the roles may alternate, with the patient sometimes assuming the role of the imagining parent and the analyst cast as the imagined child.

Deception in its various forms has been viewed in terms of the lie that is put forward and the truth that is concealed. In imposture, for example, an idealized self and a family romance are substituted for a devalued self and a history of trauma and neglect (Greenacre, 1958). Lying in analysis may serve as a resistance to the recognition of oedipal material (Weinshel, 1979) and particularly the reality of the tie between the parents (Britton, 1998). Deception has also been considered in relation to psychic organization. Kernberg (1992) places psychopathic transferences in a sequence with paranoid and depressive transferences; while I have linked different forms of deception with different levels of psychic organization (LaFarge, 1995); and Gediman (1985) has argued that imposture serves different functions at different levels of psychic organization. Lying and deception have also been considered in terms of the relation with reality (Greenacre, 1958; LaFarge, 1995), the vicissitudes of aggression (Kernberg, 1992; LaFarge, 1995), and the destruction of the link of understanding between self and other (Bion, 1962).

As I have attempted over many years to work clinically with deceptive patients, I have found it most useful to consider deception as a particular solution to the narcissistic struggle over the control of reality. From this perspective, the activities of deception, in which one person controls and manipulates another's experience of reality, involve the enactment of specific kinds of fantasies of imaginer and imagined. A clinical focus upon these fantasies as they emerge in transference and countertransference, helps to organize the disturbing and confusing clinical situations that arise with deceptive patients. From a theoretical standpoint, fantasies of imaginer and imagined may be seen as a framework in which the deceiver brings together and manages wishes and conflicts surrounding the experience of self and the relation of self to reality, and the vicissitudes of aggression.

When we look at deceptive patients in this way, it is possible to place the dynamics of deception along a continuum with the dynamics of other forms of narcissism. At one end we can locate the group of nondeceptive narcissistic patients for whom the fantasy of imaginer and imagined is fundamentally one of *authentication*: that is, these patients remain stably identified with the imagined self and turn to the figure of the imagining parent to define the self and bolster a sense of authenticity. Next on the continuum are those patients for whom the figure of the imagining other serves more complex functions, and may be more distorted or split; patients in this group also retain a dominant identification with the imagined self, but may on occasion reverse roles. Continuing further along, we find patients engaged in *imposture*, in which the patient maintains a split fantasy of imaginer and imagined and is simultaneously identified with the imagined child on the positive side of the split and the imagining parent on the negative side. Finally, at the far end, we find the phenomenon of *malicious deception*, in which the patient is primarily identified with the hostile annihilating imagining parent on the dark side of the split, placing the object in the role of a helpless, annihilated imagined child. Although I have placed different types of patients at specific points on my continuum, I think it is clear that a patient might fall between the points I have sketched or move back and forth along the continuum at different moments.

First Clinical Vignette: Authentication

Let me begin by presenting material from a nondeceptive patient, whose narcissistic pathology falls relatively near the pole of authentication on the continuum I have sketched. Mrs. P[1], a married woman in her thirties, presented for treatment with the complaint that she felt shadowy and inauthentic. She felt that she did not know herself and feared that there was no solid self for her to know. She turned to others in external reality and in fantasy in order to discover her self, seeing herself as she thought her mother or father would see her. Her parents' wishes and views of her were themselves patchy and contradictory, and Mrs. P's sense of herself often felt assembled like a collage, a figure without a core. Mrs. P felt that her marriage was happy; she was successful at her work; but somehow little of her being came alive in a steady way.

Mrs. P was an only child, born to parents whose sense of themselves also seemed, in her description, to be filmy and insecure. Her father had been very uncertain of his own identity, and both parents appeared to have rewritten their identities to omit terrible experiences earlier in their lives.

Early in her analysis, Mrs. P presented a dream that was to become a leitmotif for our work together: In the dream, she left a dangerous landscape to go aboard a train that ran through a long chute or tunnel. Once on the train, Mrs. P's view of the world outside was blocked; she had access only to artificial dioramas that were painted on the walls of the tunnel.

Mrs. P's telling of this dream was accompanied by a shift in both the quality and the content of her associations, and it acted to engage *me* in a different kind of relationship. Previously, Mrs. P had associated smoothly. Although she spoke about fears concerning me and the analysis, she never seemed overwhelmed; she talked about being afraid that she would lose her bearings, but she never actually did so. Similarly, I was generally able to listen in a steady way, to resonate with what she said without being swept away myself.

Now, when Mrs. P finished reporting her dream, she found herself suddenly unable to think; she felt drugged, stupefied, and without words. As I listened to her stumbling, anxious speech, I also felt ungrounded, as if I were pressured to put things together, to think for both of us, but unable to do more than point out how anxious Mrs. P must be feeling. Recovering, Mrs. P observed that she had had an "Alice in Wonderland feeling." She resumed her associations to the dream, ending the session with the recollection that she had recently read a magazine story where there was a chute just like the one in the dream. The story had been about an autistic woman, Temple Grandin, who was interviewed by Oliver Sacks. Grandin had devised the chute to convey animals into the slaughterhouse while protecting them from awareness of their terrible destination.

Returning to the dream in the following session, Mrs. P said that she thought Temple Grandin represented me; the dream was about what I was supposed to do in analysis—make her a safe place where she would be protected from anxiety.

I objected that this would not be any real help. Nothing would be changed. All the same dangers would still be there. She would just be unaware of them. And worse still, if I was Temple Grandin, I would be leading her into danger even while I was shielding her from the knowledge of it!

Mrs. P disagreed. This was just what she wanted from me. In fact, if I looked at the things in her head and told her that they were fine, then they *were* fine! That would be great! For the first time, she said, she felt helped by the analysis. She was now able to settle in.

In the terms I have laid out, Mrs. P's dream of Temple Grandin marked the crystallization in the transference of a central fantasy of imaginer and imagined. This was a fantasy in which Mrs. P, the imagined child, would come to know herself *exclusively* through the vision of a highly idiosyncratic imagining parent, Temple Grandin. Mrs. P would surrender her own perceptions entirely to this parent; whatever sense of self she acquired, she would gain through the experience of being known, even wrongly known.

Mrs. P's fantasy of imaginer and imagined took the general form of a fantasy of *authentication*: that is, it was a fantasy in which Mrs. P, identified with the imagined child, discovered who she was through the vision of an imagining parent, represented as Temple Grandin. We can see that the situation was considerably more complex than that. One might argue that the self that was authenticated for Mrs. P in her fantasy was hardly an authentic one— that Temple Grandin incorporates little of Mrs. P's subjective experience in her dioramas. And such a fantastical, complicated internalized figure as Temple Grandin clearly must serve a host of functions in Mrs. P's mental life, shaping Mrs. P's sense of herself and her objects in accord with Mrs. P's wishes and defensive needs. Nevertheless, Mrs. P's fantasy centers on the acquisition of a sense of self through the agency of another.

If we look at Mrs. P's early transference in this way, we can see that the analyst working with her—and with other patients for whom fantasies of imaginer and imagined center on *authentication*—faces two central tasks. First, she must uncover the specific fantasies of the imagining parent that emerge in the transference and countertransference, and come to understand their meanings and functions. What does it mean for me to be shielding Mrs. P from the knowledge of danger at the same time as I lead her into it? And what are the dangers from which Mrs. P wishes to be shielded? Are all intense affects felt to be dangerous, or is anger the main danger? Where does sexuality come into it? Does the impression of *generalized* danger actually hide the dangers of *specific* wishes that Mrs. P does not wish to see? Why does Mrs. P believe that change occurs only through magic and not through her own agency?

At the same time, the analyst must explore a second, often hidden line of inquiry: Why does Mrs. P choose to know herself only through another person? What has happened to her capacity for direct experience and self-knowledge? Why must she surrender these?

Like other patients for whom authentication is a central wish, Mrs. P exerted a strong pull on me to play out a version of analysis in which I would do the thinking and organizing for her. At first she would present me with *extra-analytic* emergencies that required my input; then, as the analysis proceeded, she would find herself unable to think when a new *internal* conflict began to emerge. Often she would remain calm and unmoved while stirring in me the anger and fear that she herself might otherwise have felt. It was important for me to maintain a reflective attitude about the *way* that Mrs. P and I were constructing a narrative together, as well as the *content* of the narrative that we constructed.

Despite this pull toward enactment, it was possible for Mrs. P's analysis to progress in a steady and productive way, and Mrs. P and I were generally able to experience ourselves as collaborators. After a period of several years during which the analytic work focused on the evolving series of imagining parents that emerged in transference and countertransference, and the many meanings that each of these figures had for Mrs. P, gradually this organization of experience began to give way, and Mrs. P began to understand the many reasons why she had relied on this indirect form of self-knowledge. These included her fear that her own self-experience would bring her into violent conflict with her parents; the tremendous disloyalty and guilt that she felt when she saw things her own way and her fear that she would lose her parents' love if she did so; and finally, her wish to escape from the full intensity and dangerousness of her own conflictual experience.

Mrs. P was *not* a deceptive patient. As we move along the continuum I have drawn, such a steady collaboration is much less possible. For deceptive patients of all kinds, the construction of an analytic narrative—of a story of who the patient is and how his life evolved—tends to be marked by dramatic shifts in the experience of reality for analyst, patient, or both.

Second Clinical Vignette: Imposture

My second example is from the treatment of an imposturous patient, Mr. F[2] Mr. F, an attractive, well dressed, generally well-spoken man in his late 20s, presented for treatment with a romantic dilemma. He was seeing two women and was unsure which of the two he wished to marry. As Mr. F told me about himself and his history, I felt sympathetic. I liked Mr. F If I had been interviewing him for a high-level job, I would have hired him. As he began to tell me in detail about the two women and his relationships with them though, I had difficulty forming a clear picture of either of them, or distinguishing between them. I asked him to tell me how they differed from each other.

Mr. F. sketched two shapes in the air with his hands. "Susie is like *this*," he said, drawing a curvy outline, "And Jane is like *that*!" He sketched two straight lines. I must have experienced some discomfort with Mr. F's verbal description of his two amours, or else I would not have asked my question. Nevertheless, I was stunned by his response. Mr. F's object world was clearly much cruder than I had thought! He did not appear to be joking. Mr. F did not signal in any way that his hand gestures might be odd or out of the context of his elaborate verbal narrative. Rather he conveyed the sense that he had simply continued his spoken story in an unremarkable way. He now returned to talking more abstractly about women and relationships.

As Mr. F continued with his narrative, my former feeling of engagement and sympathy returned. Mr. F now told me something of his life story. He had grown up in a large, fairly prosperous family on the eastern seaboard. On a family trip to Europe, a chance encounter with Prince Rainier and Princess Grace had led to a lasting relationship. He had become almost an adoptive son to them, returning to visit them in Monaco. In fact his fluency in French as well as many of his values and political beliefs originated in that remarkable relationship.

As I listened to this story, my sympathy and interest in Mr. F only increased. What an unusual man he was! Clearly, as I recount it to you now, Mr. F's tale of his adoption by Prince Rainier is outrageous, a caricature of a family romance, and yet, as I listened to him tell it, and for several months thereafter, I believed this story unquestionably to be true. Indeed the attitude of belief that Mr. F evoked in me was so powerful that it exerted the same effect when I told his story to others. At a clinical seminar where I presented his case, the conclusion of the group was that Mr. F must have been a remarkable boy for a royal figure to have taken such an interest in him.

How can we understand the events of my first meeting with Mr. F? From one perspective, we could say that Mr. F communicated to me three stories more or less in the following sequence: The first was the story Mr. F told me about his coming to see me as a patient and about his relationships with women and the problems he had with them. This story was told in words, and was the kind of story that we usually think of as true. Then in the middle of the session, Mr. F communicated another story about women, this one in gestures. This was a story of women being nothing but bodies for him, barely distinguishable from one another. Finally, Mr. F told me another story in words. This was a fantastical family romance, and although I believed it when I heard it, it was not on the face of it very credible.

This sequence puts the material of the session in order, and in that sense is more organized than my experience of the session as I lived it, when Mr. F's dramatic gesture first stunned me and then quickly faded from my awareness. But this way of looking at the session does not really get to the heart of the matter. Why did I drop my recognition of Mr. F's crudeness as soon as he resumed his spoken story? And why did I believe his preposterous story of Prince Rainier, which was so clearly false, a caricature of a family romance? These are the questions that are at the center of what it means to be Mr. F, or to be with Mr. F.

I think that we can grasp the session best if we imagine that Mr. F was playing out with me simultaneously both sides of a split fantasy of imaginer and imagined. In the first fantasy—he idealized one side of the split—Mr. F, who is identified with the role of the imagined child, presents me with wishful stories of himself that become real for him when I, in the role of the imagining parent, accept and confirm them. Thus through my listening, Mr. F feels himself to be truly a suffering, conflicted lover who is struggling with his fate, and then, more fantastically, is reassured of his remarkable "adoption" and the unique personal qualities that led to it. Mr. F plays his part in this fantasy and draws me into mine by the charming, convincing way he tells his tale and assumes the role of the hero of it. He maintains an air of illustriousness and at the same time looks to me for my opinion about the "problems" he brings to me for help.

In the second enactment, the negative side of the split fantasy is played out, and our roles are reversed. Now Mr. F is identified with the imagining parent while I am cast in the role of the imagined child. The kind of listening and imagining that Mr. F does is entirely destructive. Far from playing the role of a parent who confirms the child's subjective experience, he acts to invalidate my experience entirely. Mr. F carries out this part of the enactment by acting as if evidence that contradicts his illustrious tone does not exist— or if it does exist, has no bearing on his favored story—signaling to me that I too am to dismiss the parts of my perceptions that do not fit—my amazement at his primitivity and my potential suspicion of his tall tale.

Both of these storylines are being played out at all times during the session but it is easier to see each of them at a different moment. Mr. F's spoken stories, which engage me so sympathetically, show us how much he wishes to discover an idealized version of himself in my eyes; while his utter dismissal of any significance that his hand gestures might have either for himself or for me demonstrate the pressure that he puts on me to disavow my own perceptions in favor of his preferred version of reality.

What was my contribution to this complicated enactment? Certainly Mr. F was compelling, but why did I fall in so easily with his imposture? Kris (2005) has described the way our own tendency toward splitting and our wish for a tie with an idealized object draw us into believing the liar's tales. Mr. F was certainly a better, more wished-for patient in the persona of adoptee and romantic hero than in his role as liar and sexual exploiter. In addition, the huge discrepancy in level of organization between Mr. F's imposturous performance and the primitive parts of himself, which he signaled me not to see, pulled me toward the construction of a story from which the more primitive bits were omitted.[3] I will return to this in my third example.

How can the analyst work successfully with an imp"osturous patient like Mr. F? My own experience with Mr. F was certainly disappointing. In a twice-weekly psychotherapy that extended for five years, Mr. F made changes in his life that afforded him significant happiness—he married Susie and felt that their marriage was quite happy; he achieved public success in his work—but his hollowness and deceptiveness appeared to me to be unchanged. In effect, we remained throughout in the same transference and countertransference positions that appeared in the first session.

I found that it was impossible for Mr. F to form an attachment to me—or at least to acknowledge an attachment—in any role other than his imposturous one. Over the years, almost every element of the compelling story that Mr. F told me proved to be a lie. The Rainiers were the first to go. Later, when a particularly low moment in Mr. F's life led his parents to come to town and join us for a family session, I found that they were not prosperous and not from the eastern seaboard; Mr. F's father was not employed in the field Mr. F had said. Mr. F met each new exposure with the same dismissal that had marked his attitude toward his hand gestures in the first session. "Oh that about the eastern seaboard!" he seemed to say. "Yes, I said that once."

Over time, I became a figure in Mr. F's deceptions—as I would learn from others that he would miss work because of factitiously scheduled appointments with me, or be too distraught to function after a "powerful" session. At times I was also the victim of his lies. Sometimes the lies—about his finances and insurance—were subtle and were uncovered only after some time had elapsed, or, perhaps never uncovered at all. At other times, Mr. F would tell transparent, bald-faced lies, leaving a message on my answering machine to cancel a session and saying that he was calling a day earlier than he actually was.

If Mr. F was treatable, and I am not sure that he was, perhaps it was my inability to tolerate the full emotional experience of being lied to by him that led to the failure of his therapy to deepen. Clearly Mr. F wanted to hurt me with many of his lies, yet looking back I am struck by how little I *felt* hurt. With each new revelation, I felt amazed once again at Mr. F's ways, identifying more with his prowess and daring as a liar than with my own victimization and anger. In addition, I think, the emotional experience of being lied to by Mr. F would have entailed a closer contact with the discontinuous, even disorganized quality that Mr. F's own experience likely had—the spaces in between the islands of his polished narrative.

Third Clinical Vignette: Malicious Deception

In my work with another patient, the experience of being lied to did come alive for me more fully.[4] Miss A was a patient whose analysis was very satisfying to me for a number of years. Sadistic and masochistic themes were prominent in the analysis, but Miss A appeared to work very well with them. Her rich associations unfolded with unusual clarity, and my interpretations often led to further deepening. She moved back and forth between the transference and events outside the analysis. Insights achieved in the analysis of the transference led over time to significant life change.

After a year or two, I became aware that I had an unusual, steady countertransference to Miss A: As I listened to her, the characters and scenes that she described came alive for me in a stream of visual imagery. I never felt disengaged from Miss A, but I never really felt thrown by her either. This was particularly surprising because Miss A's level of psychopathology seemed to me to be quite severe; her associations were often quite violent; and the figure of the mother that emerged in both her memories and the transference was one of an intrusive paranoid woman who was at times openly psychotic.

The intense reactions of a peer supervisory group to whom I presented my work with Miss A confirmed my sense that I somehow shielded myself from the full impact of Miss A's aggression. With the group's support, I was able to allow aggressive and paranoid material to emerge more fully in transference and countertransference. I now felt frightened of and for Miss A at times, and was fearful as well for the survival of the analysis. Still the process that we had established righted itself after each disruption. My sense was that I knew Miss A intimately, and I think she would have said that she felt deeply known by me.

Late in the analysis, Miss A told me that she had committed a serious financial indiscretion at work. Without telling me, over a number of weeks she had dishonestly manipulated funds. Now changes in the business climate threatened her with exposure. I reeled as I listened to Miss A. I was overwhelmed with anxiety, terrified of the real potential consequences of her behavior, and disturbed by her self destructiveness and her keeping this secret from me.

As the days passed, Miss A's sessions were filled with her descriptions of the practical problems she was facing and the way she was dealing with them, the lawyer she consulted, and so on. My anxiety rose to a crescendo. I opened the morning paper each day afraid that I would read of Miss A's arrest. My own fate seemed bound up and even blurred with hers as I imagined that Miss A would publicly blame her crime on my deficient understanding and help.

After two weeks, Miss A announced with great pleasure that the whole story of the financial manipulation had been a fabrication! She had wanted to frighten me and control my mind! She had purposely selected for her fabrication an area in which she had correctly sensed that she had expertise and I did not. Her associations went to her own experiences with a psychotic mother who entrapped her in a paranoid view of reality. Miss A traced the timing of her cruel hoax to my recent vacation. After many years when she had minimized her reactions to separations, she had become aware how angry she was at my absences. Likely she had also wanted to make me suffer as she had suffered at her mother's hands. I was staggered by the immense cruelty of Miss A's behavior toward me. Although it was comprehensible to me in the light of her early history, I could not really integrate it with any transference events that had preceded it. After some time it ceased to be the focus of our sessions, but it remained an isolated, highly disturbing event.

A year later developments in the analysis led to a further understanding of Miss A's cruel lie. Miss A now felt ready to set a termination date. As she contemplated leaving me, she reflected that throughout the analysis she had not existed as a separate person. In fantasy, she had felt that her body had been encased within my body, and her thoughts had been encased within my thoughts. It was as if, for Miss A, I thought all her thoughts along with her, in perfect synchrony. I was always with her in the process of her thinking, and we always shared a single view.

As Miss A described her sense of existing so smoothly and steadily inside me, I was able to link her fantasy to my countertransference experience of overly smooth and steady listening. Throughout the long course of her analysis, Miss A had engaged me in enacting a fantasy in which I served as a steady imagining parent who knew her perfectly and never argued with her over her subjective experience. Within the frame of my listening presence, Miss A had been able to elaborate a story of her self that was quite complex and durable. I played different roles *within* this story, and the story included areas of conflict between Miss A and myself, but we did not fight about the *construction* of the story. Here we were in perfect harmony.

If the productive collaboration that Miss A had enjoyed with me had reflected an idealized fantasy of being encased in my understanding, her dramatic lie reflected the negative side of the same split fantasy, as well as a reversal of roles. Now Miss A took the role of a cruel imagining parent who encased *me* within *her* thinking, terrifying me as she spun a convincing lie that undermined my own capacity to perceive and reflect.

As Miss A and I looked back on the meaning that our smooth collaboration had had for her, we could see that the cruelty and rage that surfaced in her lie were the inevitable byproduct of the idealization that had dominated the analysis. Unconsciously, Miss A had tailored herself to my knowing her, leaving out both parts of herself that she felt I would not understand and, in addition, her repeated experiences of being misunderstood by me. If she had consciously felt perfectly understood by me, she had also felt, in a split-off part of her experience that I failed to know or understand her, and, as her anger grew, that I was willfully forcing her to fit within my vision of her and angrily repudiating the parts of her that did not fit. Finally, with her malicious lie, she had assumed the role of this cruel, misimagining parent and forced me to take the role of the frightened, misimagined child. In fantasy, with her malicious lie, Miss A had done to me exactly what she felt that *I* had done to *her*.

This new understanding enabled Miss A to work productively during a long termination phase, and ultimately to separate from me. However, our analytic work by no means resolved the split in Miss A's experience of self and imagining object. She remained vulnerable to further serious regressions in the years that followed. Looking back at our work together, I have wondered if Miss A, like Mr. F, was ultimately untreatable, or alternately, if my capacity to work with her was limited by my ability to tolerate earlier in the analysis the full emotional impact of the transferences that she brought to the treatment. As with Mr. F, these intolerable, or barely tolerable transferences would include the massive aggression that accompanied her attack on my experience of reality—an experience of which I had as much as I could take during the period of her cruel hoax—and, more subtly, the underlying sense of disorganization and discontinuity—possibly of psychotic experience—that stand at the edge of the more brightly lit dramas that these patients bring forward.

Discussion

As we follow the continuum that I have drawn from authentication through imposture to malicious deception, we encounter patients who are difficult or even impossible to treat analytically. Deceptive patients are notoriously challenging for the therapist or analyst. Kernberg (1984) considers the presence of psychopathic features to be an indication that a narcissistic patient is unsuitable for psychoanalysis. He has described better results in psychotherapy with such patients, and has depicted a characteristic sequence of transference unfolding in these cases, in which psychopathic transferences are succeeded first by the paranoid transferences which, he believes, are their mirror image, and then by depressive transferences (1992). My own clinical experience with this group of patients (both those I have treated myself in psychotherapy and psychoanalysis, and those whose treatment I have supervised) has been quite mixed and does not give me powerful grounds for optimism. Different problems arise with each group and with each mode of treatment.

For the imposturous patients whom I have treated the thinness and hollowness of the transference relationship have been central problems. For these patients, who are simultaneously identified with an idealized false self, on one side of a split fantasy of imaginer and imagined, and with an imagining parent who demands the surrender of the child's perceptions on the other, the analytic or therapeutic process is undone even as it occurs. It is never wholly real for the patient, and often for the analyst as well. It is useful to consider in each case the dominant functions that imposture serves, and particularly its relationship to aggression. Is the main gain the confirmation of a wished-for view of self? Is material gain involved? That is, does the impostor make use of his false self to extract from his objects? Is harming the object in fact the main aim? These factors, which tell us something about the qualities of the fantasy of the aggressive imagining parent with whom the impostor is identified, help to locate an imposture along the continuum leading to malicious deception.

In the treatment of patients who present the problem of malicious deception, the most serious problem that arises in treatment has to do with the intense aggression that emerges and must be tolerated by both patient and analyst, or therapist. Like other identifications with a powerful sadistic object (Rosenfeld, 1971; Kernberg, 1984), the liar's identification with the sadistic imagining parent can be contained in an analytic, or even a therapeutic process only if it is episodic, a regressive potential that emerges only after a significant period of treatment, as it did with Miss A, and is not a chronic, organizing stance. Even in this case, the emergence of the sadistic lie reflects a fault line in personality organization and a seam of primitive aggression and vengefulness that is not easily or fully resolved (Schafer, 2005; LaFarge, 2006).

Both impostorous and psychopathic transferences may serve as defensive organizations that ward off higher-level oedipal and depressive conflict. However, deceptive phenomena also serve to screen more primitive fragmentation and psychotic experience. Thus impostorous patients and patients who lie maliciously often evoke in the analyst countertransference anxieties related to disorganization and psychotic experience. Faced with the patient's discontinuous, even fragmented experience, the analyst tends to mobilize his own capacity for organization, joining with the patient, as I did with both Mr. F and Miss A, to spin a story that hangs together and excludes disturbing, alien elements that do not fit.

How should we select a treatment for deceptive patients? If analysis brings us closer to them and allows us to understand them more fully, it also exposes these fragile patients to the danger of further regression. Conversely however, those patients who have been able to tolerate psychoanalysis with me have formed an attachment that has anchored them and permitted them to return to me at difficult times long after termination. Once again, I think, the quality and dominance of the patient's identification with the figure of the aggressively imagining parent is an important indicator. At best, we can treat in psychoanalysis only those patients for whom the representation of the mis-imagining parent is not too sadistic and the patient's identification with this figure is not complete or chronic. Deceptive patients, who themselves strive to transform reality along the lines of their wishes, may induce in the therapist or analyst a parallel sense of omnipotence. It is possible that for many deceivers, we may be most helpful if we accompany them as closely as we can in their jagged, often tragic course without expecting that we will be able to render it as smooth and steady as we might like.

Notes

1. I have described Mrs. P's analysis more fully in "On knowing oneself directly and through others" (LaFarge, 2008).

2. I have discussed Mr. F. briefly in my paper "Transferences of deception" (1995).

3. Greenacre (1958) has observed the contrast between the impostor's "two dominant identities . . . the temporarily focused and strongly assertive imposturous one, and the frequently amazingly crude and poorly knit one from which the impostor has emerged" (p. 97–98).

4. I have described this case more fully in "The wish for revenge" (LaFarge, 2006).

References

Bion, W.R. (1962). *Learning From Experience*. London: Karnac.

Britton, R. (1998). *Belief and Imagination*. London: Routledge.

Gediman, H. (1985). Imposture, inauthenticity and feeling fraudulent. *Journal of the American Psychoanalytic Association* 33: 911–993.

Greenacre, P. (1958). The impostor. In: *Emotional Growth, Vol. 1*, pp. 93–112. New York: International Universities Press, 1971.

Kernberg, O. (1984). *Severe Personality Disorders*. New Haven, CT: Yale University Press.

Kernberg, O. (1992). Psychopathic, paranoid and depressive transferences. *International Journal of Psychoanalysis* 73: 13–28.

Kris, A.O. (2005). The lure of hypocrisy. *Journal of the American Psychoanalytic Association* 53: 7–22.

LaFarge, L. (1995). Transferences of deception. *Journal of the American Psychoanalytic Association* 43: 765–792.

LaFarge, L. (2004). The imaginer and the imagined. *Psychoanalytic Quarterly* 73: 591–625.

LaFarge, L. (2006). The wish for revenge. *Psychoanalytic* Quarterly 75: 447–475.

LaFarge, L. (2008). On knowing oneself directly and through others. *Psychoanalytic Quarterly* 77: 167–197.

Rosenfeld, H. (1971). A clinical approach to the psychoanalytic theory of the life and death instincts: an investigation into the aggressive aspects of narcissism. *International Journal of Psychoanalysis* 52: 169-178.

Schafer, R. (2005). Cordelia, Lear, and forgiveness. *Journal of the American Psychoanalytic Association* 53: 389–409.

Weinshel, E. (1979). Some observations on not telling the truth. *Journal of the American Psychoanalytic Association* 27: 503–531.

CHAPTER FIVE

~

Where Does the Truth Lie?

Harold P. Blum, M.D.

Dr. Lucy LaFarge, in her fascinating paper "Authentication, Imposture, and Malicious Deception" illuminates thorny, perplexing issues with theoretical and clinical acuity. Dr. LaFarge is very sensitive to the patient's verbal and non-verbal associations, her own responses, and the patient's response or lack of response to her interventions and interpretations. We quickly grasp how she analytically confronts her own pleasure in analytic work, as well as confusion, irritation, and disappointment, her anxiety and anger. The effect of the deceptive patient on the countertransference is openly, clearly addressed. Important issues in the treatment of liars appear in relief. What kind of treatment is best for the type of patient with particular problematic types of deception? Is the patient suitable for analysis when "lying on the couch," or for analytic psychotherapy, counseling, family theory, pharmacological treatment, and so forth? Many pathological liars do not seek treatment or readily leave treatment; within treatment they present extraordinary challenges.

Lucy LaFarge's Contribution

Dr. LaFarge places these patients on a continuum of minor to major narcissistic personality disorder, a framework that organizes and enlarges our understanding of the patient's character and psychopathology. The patients' narcissistic disorder is highlighted in the here and now transference-countertransference field as well as in their current object relations and life situation. Lucy LaFarge is not theoretically or technically seduced into an all-transference orientation in which the patient's narcissism is bolstered and gratified in an imaginary analytic situation in which the analyst or therapist is the only significant object in the patient's life. Her emphasis on narcissism and narcissistic relationships is very relevant and helpful. At the same time I was intrigued and challenged by what was not mentioned, conspicuous by its absence. This is a very original presentation on lying, the first I have encountered that did not refer to the superego and to superego lacunae, superego malformation, superego regression, dysfunction, disharmony, and so forth. Associated guilt and shame are also, regrettably, not discussed. The different perspectives, narcissism and superego, are very significant; they are usually complementary rather than incompatible perspectives. Except in the most extreme forms of psychopathology, narcissistic issues and superego considerations coexist and are closely interrelated, for example in the concept of the ego ideal. Our understanding should be enriched through consideration of these theoretical and developmental perspectives and their clinical application. There are innumerable clinical pictures and permutations. An individual may feel above the law, narcissistically omnipotent and invulnerable. He can consort with prostitutes while lying to his spouse, yet still have an unconscious need for punishment and humiliation. Another person's so-called crime of passion, a murder and its attempted cover-up, may be selectively permitted to avenge and undo narcissistic injuries and oedipal defeat, while incest may remain strictly forbidden. A martinet may project guilt and self-criticism onto others, contributing to the grandiose illusion of the near perfect self.

The representations described by Dr. LaFarge of the imagining and the imagined have complementary and supplementary reality concerns. Dr. La-Farge perceptively interprets the unconscious motive of her less disturbed patients to have their knowledge and testing of reality authenticated, and I may also add to consolidate an authentic identity. The ever-present interaction of external and psychic reality is too easily obscured in the confusion and perplexities introduced by the true or false as well as true and false information given by devious, dishonest patients. Lies are communicated at many different developmental levels (Gediman, 1985). It should also be noted that there are many over-determined motives, and various types of liars and forms of lies. There are big liars, and there are little fibbers. In clinical work, how do we believe a word that we have heard? We expect that a patient who reports his/her age, marital status, number of children, occupation, and other basic existential realities is being factual. If they lie about anything and everything, they are untreatable by dynamic psychotherapy, and most likely are refractory to any form of treatment. There are patients who rarely lie, who only occasionally lie, or who tell little fibs or white lies, but are not generally mendacious. Contrary to pathogenic dishonesty, white lies may serve social and reality adaptation; lies may serve safety and survival under conditions of persecution. Children reared with harsh punishments rather than appropriate discipline are more likely to be evasive and deceptive.

Further Phenomenological Details

Some patients present half-truths, or lie only about details (though the devil may be in the details) with or without malice aforethought. There are habitual liars, compulsive liars, liars who also believe their own lies, liars who tell sequences of lies upon lies. There is a range from embellishing, boasting and bragging, to gross exaggeration, to ornamental fabrication, to the malignant con artist. Highly skilled and practiced liars may appear to have carried deliberate deception to an art form, as in the case of the "con artist" gaining the confidence of the gullible victim. The "confidence man" gains the confidence of the gullible victim, with sadism hidden behind a façade of narcissistic charm and charisma. The con artist and swindler gratify their infantile greed and confirm their characterological omnipotence through their material reward at the painful expense of their victim. Lies deny unpleasant truths, and may screen earlier traumatic memories distorted in unconscious fantasy (Deutsch, 1939). The lie conceals and partly reveals the truth. A tissue of lies, as in pseudologia fantastica, is often interwoven with reality in a compromise formation of fact and fantasy (Fenichel, 1954). There is a grain of truth in every delusion (Freud, 1937). Motives for lying involve the whole of developmental challenges and unconscious and conscious conflict. The more psychopathic liar, narcissistic, and with a deformed superego, may give his/her word of honor to seduce the witness. The deceived witness is drawn into unconscious collusion, an aspect of a transference-countertransference bind in analysis and psychotherapy.

The development of symbolic, linguistic, affective, and cognitive capacities for pretense, pretend play, and anticipation of consequences in the second year foreshadow the later appearance of the conscious, intentional lie. The toddler can play "I will leave you and you will leave me" with imagined roles and role reversals before more complex imaginary constructions of plot and dialogue (Neubauer, 1987) involved in lying. Pretend play is dissociated from external reality, and represents imaginary organizations of ideas, affects, controlled symbolic actions, and social role rehearsal. Pretend play requires a parent who can confidently, pleasurably play with the child, and who validates the child's reality testing, and separate identity, and who fosters individuation

(Winnicott, 1971). Language and advancing verbal communication facilitate reality adaptation, but may be deployed and derailed toward misleading messages and deceptive narration. Children begin to overtly lie at approximately three years of age, lying to others and to themselves in self-deception. Differentiated from truth, lying may be regarded as a developmental achievement, a learned ability, accomplished with greater facility in the more intelligent child (Talwar et al., 2007). Freud (1913) noted the wishful fantasies in the benign lies of children, comparing the lies to the myths and legends of nations. Freud concurrently observed children lying in identification with lying parents. The toddler has a greater grasp of reality than earlier in infancy, and can begin to construct an "alternate reality" in fantasy. Most three and four year olds will lie to avoid blame, for example, denying that they hit a sibling or overturned a glass, even when the parent observed the action. Lies are frequently related to avoiding, restoring, and repairing narcissistic injury, to raising self-esteem, to avoid punishment or to unconsciously seek punishment. The child who invents or exaggerates abilities and accomplishments wishes to be the idealized adult, to become the ideal, aggrandized self, the hero or heroine of a family romance. Wishful thinking, magically undoing disappointments, narcissistic injuries and traumas, and the greater reliance of children on defenses of denial, splitting, and role reversal sets the stage for magical tricks of pretense, deception, guile, and lies. The child who has experienced parental lying may seek revenge for having been deceived. In the case of Little Hans (Freud, 1909) the boy resented his father's fabrication that the stork brought his baby sister. Through emulation and identification some children will become adolescents who have developed lying into a familial psychodrama. Children and adolescents will typically lie to preserve autonomy and parental approval (Blum and Blum, 1990) as well as to avoid unpleasant truths and consequences. An adolescent may lie about truancy, drugs, sex, and so on while believing lying is wrong. Lies may ambivalently conceal the transgressions of others, such as parents, sibs, and close friends. An adolescent patient reported that her mother was much more proficient at lying than herself, but that an aunt was the champ. Another patient extrapolated lying into financial manipulations at the border of fraud. While some of these individuals feel validated and exonerated when others lie to them, many are outraged and believe they have been double-crossed. King Lear demanded flattery and was later enraged by pretended affection. There are personality disorders who appear to have "multiple super-egos" with inconsistent, often contradictory standards and values, and/or deficient capacities for shame and guilt. Some so-called shameless individuals may have unconscious guilt or an unconscious fear of retaliation. In some patients the superego seems lax, easily bribed, and readily modified or mollified by new identifications. For the malignant narcissistic personality, narcissistic need and entitlement, co-opting ideals and values, have long surpassed ethical concerns.

Lying, false premises and promises are often socially sanctioned by and in group process. In the political world there is a range and intertwining of frequent mendacity in the service of social, political, and economic propaganda to malicious fabrication, and distortion of reality. In the group of two, the analytic dyad as the disguised realm of the imagined child of the imagining parent, and the shared fantasy system of a 'folie a deux' cannot be fully comprehended without the child's selective identifications with the parents. A psychotic parent's pathogenic influence on the child's conflicts and development may be inferred in the transference and in analytic reconstruction. A child may lie about the parent's psychotic state while knowing, on some level, that the parent is "crazy." The child may treat the parent with great caution and concern when the parent is disorganized, while both denying the disorder and joining the delusional system. With denial, reversal, and repression, self-deception is transformed in unconscious fantasy. The imagining parent refers to parental fantasy about the child, but without analytic reconstruction does not inform about the influence and impact of such a particular fantasy on the imagined child.

Matters of Technique

Lucy LaFarge's patients have had the benefit of treatment with a very thoughtful, empathic analyst. Each of her cases would be worthy of an extensive discussion. I can only select some salient clinical comments and questions for further elaboration. In her first case, the train traveling through the tunnel without the patient having external bearings, suggests free association and the analytic process. The free associating patient does not know the where or why of her further thoughts and feelings. Dr. LaFarge was sensitively and tactfully able to gain this difficult patient's collaboration. In the patient's nightmarish report, she was in a sealed train with restricted visibility, allowing her to see only the graffiti, what might be called "the handwriting on the wall." The patient sought reassurance that she is not being transported to her death, like an animal to the slaughterhouse. The analogy to the holocaust is powerfully implied. I wonder about her possible identification with Holocaust victims and perpetrators, and about real trauma disguised as imaginary danger. Nightmares are indicative of traumatic experience. Was the traumatic experience denied and dissociated? (Both parents had rewritten history to hide terrible experiences in childhood.) Was the patient or an object with whom she identified, deceived and tricked? Is she or her analyst the killer or victim? Many victims of the Holocaust and other massacres were deliberately deceived about their fate. Holocaust, prisoner, and child abuse victims, as well as survivors of severe childhood illness were frequently disoriented and destabilized, as they were often subjected to being deceived in a terrorized state.

Dr. LaFarge's second case was not analyzable, since he seemed indifferent to the truth, or preferred the hidden sadism of his lies. Freud (1937) stated that analysis is based on a love of truth. Freud enjoined the patient, as in a courtroom procedure, to promise to tell the truth, the whole, truth, and nothing but the truth. No editing, dismissing, or withholding of anything that came to mind. A patient who is a characteristic, chronic liar, who has little regard for fact versus fantasy is beyond analysis and is a treatment riddle. Yet this otherwise impossible patient derived benefit from treatment. Perhaps he internalized his analysis and analytic values in some corner of his warped personality; per this "as if" or psychopathic personality was able to stabilize his oscillating identifications and identify. Putting up with his deceits and conceits with patience, tolerance, and tact was likely to have been more therapeutically important than analytic insights that were disdained and rebuffed by the patient. Could he have been an imposter or accomplished liar without an accomplice parent figure in fantasy?

The third case Dr. LaFarge presented is directly relevant to a Mahler Symposium. Confronted with the analyst's separation, the patient regressed to symbiotic fantasy like a rapprochement toddler. Her object constancy was presumably fragile, and she experienced separation anxiety and separation rage when Dr. LaFarge was away. She may have projected a pregnancy fantasy of her being encased inside her analyst, or in a reversal, she retained her ambivalently regarded analyst as an unintegrated introject. However, her wish to restore a perfect mother-child intimacy on an infantile, pre-oedipal level of development seems to be an important component of the fantasy. Her putative theft could compensate for feeling cheated and deprived by her analyst's absence, and in childhood of her mother's love when her mother was paranoid. She recanted her theft, but was this related to her guilt, fear of retaliation, or fear of alienating her analyst's affection? Was she lying when she disclaimed her lie? Where does the truth lie? Had she revealed, and then denied the larceny, as occurs in criminal cases when confessions are retracted? How did her unresolved separation-individuation issues impinge on her later oedipal and adolescent development? We can only surmise the persistence of separation, object constancy, and object loss issues antecedent to post-oedipal development. Lying is not an expectable outcome of disturbed separation-individuation, and her manifest fantasy does not answer our curiosity and questions about the pathogenesis of her lying. Did a parent lie, or unconsciously both encourage and interdict dishonesty and delinquency.

An Additional Clinical Vignette

In a case of my own, pathologic lying was associated with trauma and its imaginary reversal and mastery. The case confirmed formulations of lying in order to alter and control reality. This married male in his thirties was very anxious and depressed. He accepted a recommendation for analysis after having consulted another analyst in the past who also advised psychoanalysis. Just before he was to begin analysis the patient telephoned me that his mother died and that he would contact me after the funeral. He disappeared, but then telephoned for consultation and treatment one and a half years later. At the outset he stated he had something significant to tell me. He revealed that he had fled from analysis with a false alibi. His mother had not died; it was "a big lie," later designated a "whopper." Would he lie again during the analysis, having deliberately lied for openers? Was his initial lie better understood as a symptom or character disorder? He did not lie in general. As a teen he told tall stories to his peers, exaggerating his athleticism, as though he had the mightiest bat and balls. He once filched coins from his mother's purse, but denied other theft. Neither his parents nor siblings were described as dishonest. There were, however, traumas that were treated with intrafamilial silence and evasion. His father died from cancer when the patient was ten years old. The doctor and his family concealed the cancer with white lies. After his father died the patient would play dead, only to awaken and revive. Later he dreamt his father fell off the roof and the patient as a boy caught him and pulled him back. This was the fantasy behind the big lie. He had killed me off and then resurrected me.

Death and rebirth fantasies occurred throughout his analysis. Remarking on where I was born and bred, he said "born and dead." On his sixteenth birthday a close relative committed suicide by jumping from a height. He developed obsessive thoughts of how he might have saved his relative as well as suicidal ideation. Birth and death coalesced in his revived unconscious oedipal parricidal fantasy. His father's and the relative's deaths validated his unconscious murderous fantasies engendering enormous guilt. The loss of his father was also associated with developmental strain, as well as his mother's regression. She had been episodically incontinent and often gave enemas to herself and the patient. This had never been discussed at the time, and was later rationalized as a response to organic illness. Another major earlier trauma emerged in connection with the patient's fantasies of the massacre of his family. The focus on his father's death and its aftermath served the repression and suppression of a terrifying suicide attempt or attempts of his mother when he was about four years of age. During the analysis we learned that she was identified with relatives who had been gassed in the Holocaust, and she had turned on the gas. The patient and his family could have been massacred in her suicidal-homicidal behavior. This behavior was buried in familial amnesia and white lies, ostensibly to not frighten the little boy. Because of his mother's fragility, depression, and suicidal behavior, and then his father's slow death, the patient could not express aggression toward his parents. The threat of maternal object loss and actual paternal object loss were later evaded and then denied in fantasy. He also would have preferred, he realized, that his devalued mother had died and his idealized father had lived. The object representations of both parents were compromise formations of fantasy and reality. The patient was probably a replacement child, a fantasied rebirth and resurrection of a murdered relative.

Concluding Remarks

Our object relations are always influenced by the coalescence, as well as the coexistence of the real and the imaginary. This seems to be true of happiness, which Freud thought was based on an infantile wish. The infantile wish is a component of the daydream, which all too often is also based on denial of reality. Where does the truth lie? Shakespeare illuminated these issues in his last sonnets; his incredible Sonnet 138 refers to his mistress, the gifted, promiscuous dark lady of the sonnets:

> When my love swears she is made of truth,
> I do believe her though I know she lies,
> That she might think me some untutored youth
> Unlearned in the world's false subtleties . . . .
> Thus vainly thinking that she thinks me young,
> Although she knows my days are past the best
> Simply I credit her false-speaking tongue.
> On both sides thus is simple truth suppressed.
> But wherefore says she not she is unjust?
> And wherefore say not I that I am old?
> Oh Love's best habit is in seeming trust,
> And age in love loves not to have years told.
> Therefore I lie with her, and she with me,
> And in our faults by lies we flattered be.

References

Blum, H. and Blum, E. (1990). The development of autonomy and superego precursors. *International Journal of Psychoanalysis* 71: 585–595.

Deutsch, H. (1955). The impostor. ego psychology of a type of psychopathology. *Psychoanalytic Quarterly* 24 : 483–492.

Fenichel, O. (1954). The economics of pseudologia fantastica. In: *Collected Papers of Otto Fenichel*, pp. 129–140. NewYork: International Universities Press.

Freud, S. (1909). Analysis of a phobia in a five-year old boy. *Standard Edition* 10: 3–149.

Freud, S. (1913). Two lies told by children. *Standard Edition* 12: 303–310.

Freud, S. (1937). Construction in analysis. *Standard Edition* 23: 255–269.

Gediman, H. (1985). Imposture, inauthenticity and feeling fraudulent. *Journal of the American Psychoanalytic Association* 33: 911–993.

Neubauer, P. (1987). The many meanings of play. *Psychoanalytic Study of the Child* 42: 3–10.

Talwar, V., Gordon, H., and Lee, K. (2007). Lie telling behavior in school age children. *Developmental Psychology* 43: 804–810.

Winnicott, D. (1971). *Playing and Reality*. New York: Penguin

CHAPTER SIX

~

Lying and Deceitfulness in Personality Disorders

Michael H. Stone, M.D.

Freud made the comment over a hundred years ago at a psychoanalytic congress about how important it was that someone undergoing psychoanalysis have good character. The psychiatric and psychoanalytic nosology was quite different in that era compared with our current taxonomy. Borderline—or borderland, as the term was used in the late 19th century—was a vague concept situated between the not very well delineated concepts of neurosis and psychosis. As for psychopathy, when Kraepelin used the word, it was just a translation from the Greek ("illness of the mind"). Prichard had spoken of "moral insanity" in the 1830s but he didn't mean by that phrase what it had come to mean later: something akin to our notion of antisociality or psychopathy. Instead, he meant a madness of the (emotional) *morale* (in the French sense)—closer to our idea of severe depression. So the patients we confront now—who are particularly given to *lying* and *deceitfulness*; that is, the borderline, antisocial, and psychopathic patients—were first of all not classified with those labels in the early days of psychoanalysis, and besides analysts seldom worked with such people. August Aichhorn (1925) published his famous monograph titled "The Wayward Youth." One of the young boys he interviewed had been lying about a minor theft (p. 47), so Aichhorn certainly had experience with young persons who told fibs and had to be gently encouraged to come forward with the truth. There are some allusions to dishonesty in some of the papers of Melanie Klein's daughter, Melitta Schmideberg (1959a, 1959b)—who did considerable work with delinquent adolescent girls. In the early 1950s Helene Deutsch (1955) wrote her paper on the imposter. Earlier, Hervey Cleckley (1941) had written his famous monograph on the Mask of Sanity, that laid the groundwork for the revised concept of psychopathy—one in which lying and deceitfulness are prime characteristics.

For a psychoanalyst who works exclusively with patients who are amenable to classical analysis, deceitfulness is a *terra incognita*, since these patients will customarily show the good character—including the honesty and integrity—that Freud underlined at that congress long ago. When we speak of lying and deceitfulness in this context, we mean something more pervasive and serious than the exaggerations and minimizations we encounter in work with ordinary analytic patients. Patients tend to be squeamish about revealing certain sexual inhibitions or certain practices they regard as unacceptable—and here they may minimize and evade until key resistances are overcome. Or they may puff up their accomplishments and abilities, exaggerating in order to make a good impression. Lying and deceit are different matters. Before I go further in discussing those peculiarities of communication, I should add what is a related but perhaps less malignant phenomenon; namely, the disinclination to divulge certain information. This results in withholding the truth about various matters, but does not go as far as distortion or prevarication. The sexual revolution of the 60s has left many of our patients surprisingly comfortable about revealing the details of their sexual lives—including ones that in former times were associated with great embarrassment, so much so, that we would not get to hear about them till rather late stages of the treatment. But there has been no corresponding revolution in matters of coin. The more patients earn, or have in trusts and investments, the more close-mouthed they tend to be about letting the analyst know the numbers. If one talks bout strange sexual practices or cravings, one is not giving the analyst anything—except information. But to reveal high net worth carries the risk we may increase the fee; they may be much more reluctant to part with liquid assets than with illiquid personal facts.

Among better functioning patients in either psychoanalysis or in analytically oriented intensive therapy, it is uncommon to encounter, besides the customary resistances, much more in the way of purposeful lack of candor than withholding or coyness. I had worked with a college student recently who had been exposed to a fundamentalist religious high school that had a disastrous effect on her self-confidence and self-image. She made it clear there was something that happened while at that school that she couldn't bring herself to tell me. Many sessions were spent with her smiling embarrassedly, looking away in silence—leaving me to churn through my mind the various possibilities as to what literally "unspeakable" thing had taken place there. It seemed unlikely that she, a straight-A student with a rigid moralistic character, had done anything shameful. Finally she divulged to me that one of her teachers had told her he felt she was "unworthy" (by which he meant "not religious enough") to spend a semester abroad in a religious environment that the students had come to regard as a reward. This long-drawn-out drama with such a meager ending reminded me of the famous line in Horace's "Ars Poetica"—as an example of how not to write poetry—"*de montibus exiguit mus*" (and from the mountains there came forth—a mouse).

When I think of lying and deceitfulness, in contrast, I think of my experience with two broad groups: borderline, antisocial, and psychopathic patients, and also—my forensic work with mentally-ill offenders and with violent prisoners. I understand by "lying" the deliberate, fully conscious intention of telling something that is quite untrue. By "deceitfulness" I refer to efforts these persons may make to mislead, twist a fact into something no longer a fully factual statement. Saying "I went to Harvard and graduated 'summa'" when the person never even went to college, let alone Harvard—is obviously a lie. Saying "Well, I got into Harvard, but it seemed so snobby, I decided SUNY Binghamton would be a more congenial environment"—when the real truth is that the person did get accepted to Harvard, but the family could in no way afford the tuition—is being deceitful. Clinton's famous assertion that there may have been fellatio, but there was no sex—would likewise come under this heading.

With this as prelude, I can now share with you some examples of lying and deceitfulness, spanning the range from least to most pathological, and all within the diagnostic domain I just outlined. Where pertinent, I will add comments about the implications for treatment within this range of patients and incarcerated persons. Under what circumstances is therapy of whatever sort likely to have any beneficial effects? And at what point must we acknowledge that treatment cannot hope to succeed? Parallel to this discussion: what kinds of countertransference attitudes and emotions are likely to be stirred up by the various types and degrees of mendacity we may encounter?

Narcissistic Traits in a Young Man with Borderline Personality Organization

A young man was referred to me for therapy during his last year of high school by his mother, who was concerned about his violent dreams and fantasies, coupled with his tendency to lash out at her with abusive language—sprinkled liberally with four-letter words. She was worried lest he become violent, and also worried that he might fail to graduate, owing to his getting up too late for school some days, and skipping school altogether on others—as a result of which his grades were dropping below the passing level.

In my work with him I found him a curious mixture of candor—about topics where most adolescents are reticent, and dishonest about areas in his life where openness would be expected. He spoke readily about his violent dreams and masturbatory fantasies—in many of which he killed his mother or his father. They had divorced when he was seven and had both remarried. Toward his father, he was contemptuous—because the man, having been an atheist when first married, had now become a part of an evangelical sect that believed the universe was only 6,000 years old and that the dinosaurs died out because they were too big for the Ark. He hated his stepfather, an innocuous man who had never done anything mean to him—but who had, in effect, taken him away from his mother. His mother and he had slept in the same bed after the divorce, and some inappropriate sexual touching had gone on—instigated by the mother, who at that time was lonely and depressed.

He would start most sessions telling me how everything was going well—when in fact, as I learned from his mother—he was near flunking out. He talked a better game than he played, in general, reassuring me how he was now getting to school regularly and on time. Yet I would hear from his mother that he had lain in bed most of the week, not going to classes at all. This problem did improve; he took it well when I shared with him that he hadn't been quite accurate in his reporting about school attendance and performance—and did manage to go more regularly, and finally—to graduate. Enrolled in a college not far from home, he was bitter about having to leave his old room—since his mother and stepfather were adamant about his not living with them any longer. The focus in our twice-weekly sessions was on his love-hate relationship with his mother. It seemed, to hear him talk about it, that college was going well, although he was so tardy in signing up for classes that he couldn't get in to the ones he wanted. About half way through the year, I learned from his mother that he hardly went to any of the classes he told me he was attending, and was thus failing because of nonattendance. All the while he kept telling me he was "creaming" those courses. This was the big lie. Eventually he did have to drop out. He had been depressed when I began working with him; his spirits picked up when I placed him on a low dose of an antidepressant—but then he stopped taking the medication without telling me—and became depressed once again. After resuming the antidepressant, his mood improved; he regained his usual overcheerful, ingratiating way, and has seemed to be more honest about his academic troubles. He plans to reenter classes later in the year—but I remain concerned that his need to maintain a false façade of success will nudge him once again in the direction of lying and sweeping under the rug about the important matters in his current life. I enjoy working with him; I like his candor about his darkest fantasies—but get exasperated from time to time when he sleeps through the time for a session and doesn't answer his cell phone to let me know—a problem I find quite common in his generation: they all have cell phones and no one can reach them. At such moments I get in touch via text-messaging—which he taught me how to do—and he usually responds fairly quickly.

A Woman with Borderline Personality Disorder

A single woman in her late 20s had been seriously depressed since college, and had made several serious suicide attempts. She was also bulimic, especially before her period—which was also the time of month when her suicidality increased. She had formed obsessive love preoccupations with her two previous therapists, focusing actually on their wives—her idea being that the therapist was, akin to her own style of relating, obsessively in love with his wife, to the point of not caring at all about her or ever thinking about her—except during the precious few minutes of her sessions. The anlage for this pattern was not far to seek: she was the favorite of her mother, and had survived the attempt of her jealous older sister to stab her to death when she was five. But the father was so resentful of whatever attention his wife bestowed on the three children that he interfered grossly with her maternal functions, often taking her with him—just the two of them—on long trips, so he would have her all to himself. She had been in a psychoanalytically oriented therapy thrice weekly with her previous therapist—a rhythm that she and I maintained during our work. Both the previous therapist and I traveled a great deal to conferences and lectures—all of which were nightmarish times for her, partly because of the separation itself, but equally because of her fantasy that we were accompanied by our wives, with whom we were having constant glorious sex—to the absolute disregard of her very existence. My office is in my apartment; my wife sees the students she tutors next door—and the arrangement is such that occasionally the patient would encounter my wife. This would throw her predictably into a state of panic and despair. When I first began to work with her, these episodes were so fraught with hazard that she would afterwards walk against the lights hoping a car would run her over. I used to carry a signed one-physician's certificate needed to hospitalize her involuntarily, should the emergency arise—which it did twice in the beginning months of our work. The deceitfulness in her case took the form of calling the home number when I would be away, and hanging up if she heard only a woman's voice. This signaled to her that I had gone to Europe or wherever by myself—which settled her nerves considerably. But if God forbid no one were to answer, this meant that my wife was "with me" (rather than, say, out for the afternoon, shopping)—and this would send her into a tailspin. She was also untruthful about when she had been binging, since it was very embarrassing for her to acknowledge having succumbed once again to that tendency. When she was feeling suicidal, she would ask her mother to come to New York to be with her—which her mother would do quite willingly. This gave me a hint about a deeper dynamic; namely, that her obsessive love of her former therapists, or now, of myself—was a comfortable, pleasantly heterosexual, masquerade behind which was the still greater craving for mother—a wish that was tinged with (what was for her) forbidding homosexual overtones. But that layer was one we never could get to, even after she mentioned a dream whose content suggested that dynamic. I came to feel that the only "cure" for her was to find a boyfriend and marry— so she would have someone who cared about her, thus lessening the need for a pathological attachment to her therapist, or his wife. The impediment here was her morbid fear that her once jealous sister, now married with three children (for whom my patient would often babysit), would be murderously resentful of such a personal success in her younger sister. We worked for a long time on this grossly unrealistic fantasy—until finally my patient was able to date (up to now she had sedulously avoided doing so). Some months later, she became engaged, and is now married—with four children. Another positive change that took place as her condition improved, was that she stopped spreading malicious rumors about female coworkers at her workplace, and stopped telling to others—things told her in confidence. This was another form of lying, in a sense, since there was an implied promise to hold in confidence what was told her. The malicious gossip had the goal of elevating her status in the eyes of others—only lowering their status. Once married, she no longer felt at the bottom of the social heap.

Borderline Personality Disorder with Antisocial Features

This is a more crowded category, since the combination is rather common, especially in males with borderline personality disorder (BPD). However, there is no lack of examples among more numerous women with BPD. Here are some examples.

Case 1

A single woman of twenty-five was referred to me after she had been hospitalized briefly for a suicide gesture with an overdose. This came in the wake of a rejection by a man she had been having an affair with, and whom she had hoped would ask her to marry him. She had never had sex before nor even dated before, and partly for that reason was oblivious to various warning signs that this was not a match made in heaven. He told her, for example, that she was lousy in bed after their first episode of lovemaking. Both were Hindu and had been born on the subcontinent to very traditional families. She had been raised here as one of a half dozen families from that background all living near one another. She and her identical twin sister were encouraged to study hard all through their adolescence and had never dated. Before the break-up she had been extremely clingy—which I'm sure contributed to the demise of the relationship, which would never have lasted as long as it did if she had not been so needy as to overlook his petty cruelties. After the breakup, she began stalking him—calling his office hundreds of times a week, sending dozens of voluminous e-mails per day, and calling his parents—sometimes pretending to be some other woman—vilifying their son for so outrageously mistreating his girlfriend. I told her she needed—desperately—to stop this behavior, which happened to be illegal, besides being annoying, and that could land her in big legal troubles. She would blithely assure me that she had taken my advice and ceased the calling and mailing, adding how proud I would now be of her for making this difficult step. I didn't believe her, and would hear from her parents that she had indeed continued to barrage Sanjit, as I will call him, with calls and letters. I got her to let me meet with him, and when I did—he and I worked out a plan where he was to notify me by e-mail at the end of each day about how many contacts he received from her. I also met with her sister and parents, and was in phone contact with her aunts and uncles and with Sanjit's parents and their relatives. In this was I was able to draw the wagons in a circle around her, so to say, so that she had no escape from my getting to know what she was up to. If she would tell me in a session how she hadn't called Sanjit all week—would hold up the chart I had made—a large calendar, in effect—with different colored dots representing calls, e-mails, simulated calls from "others," and so forth that she had indeed made. After several months of this monitoring, her lying diminished considerably. She actually did stop contacts with Sanjit altogether, but now went on the Internet to find other men to date—whom she tended to harass in a similar way, once any of these brief relationships ended. She tended in the main to idealize me—but could switch rapidly into screams of hatred when I confronted her about her trying to call

Sanjit or whoever—upbraiding me as though I were "on their side" and against her. I would explain that I was actually on the side of her healthier self who strove toward a more mature and meaningful relationship with men, and against the childish and petulant—and quite vengeful and crazy—self that was threatening to destroy her. There was one other man she became involved with sexually for a few months—and when that ended, the stalking resumed. That man did not wait for her harassment to abate; he called the police. At 2 AM one morning a marshall came to her door and handcuffed her, taking her overnight to jail. I was notified and came, along with her parents and an attorney, to the court for her arraignment the next morning. The judge let her go on a six-months probation—with the proviso that if she refrained from stalking during that period, the record would be erased. If she reoffended, she would land in prison for sure. Also she had to be hospitalized immediately for at least a week under my care. All this was arranged and later that day she was admitted to a hospital near my office. This was a turning point in her life. She never indulged in stalking behavior again. Some months later she met a professor some years older than she and they married. She now has a two-and-a-half-year-old son, but the marriage did not work out. Currently she is depressed, feeling pessimistic about the future, and leaves much of the child care in the hands of her parents and sister, with whom she now lives. But the lying and suicide-gestures have not been part of the picture for some time. As for the lying, I had never in my forty years of practice reached out to so many "collaterals" in an effort to parry the thrust of a patient's prevarication.

Case 2

I had occasion some years ago to work with a woman in her mid-30s—the daughter of a wealthy entrepreneur—who had had a son, now four years old, by a married man with whom she had carried on a long affair. Or that at least was her story. She was no longer with that man, but had gotten him to provide generous child-support, largely through blackmail—threatening to expose the situation to his wife. She then extracted more money from her father, telling him her ex-lover had "failed" to make the support payments he had promised. She would threaten suicide if either man were slow with the cash. Her background was free of the usual adverse factors one sees in borderline patients: no incest, no parental neglect or cruelty, though there were some relatives with affective disorder. I tried to get her to work; she got as far as taking a volunteer job with a charity organization. She lied to me about how she went to it regularly and kept good hours, when in fact she went only sporadically and did very little when she did show up. I arranged a family meeting with her, her father, her two brothers and their wives—in an effort to work out an arrangement where she gave them a fair and honest budget of her financial needs, and they in turn would give her a corresponding amount each month—with the promise she would cease trying to cadge additional sums from her father, and would stop taking money from the putative father. There was, by the way, considerable doubt as to whether the boy was actually his, but he refused DNA testing. He had no contact with the boy whatsoever. In this meeting—conducted at her father's office—all seemed to go well; she agreed to the arrangement that got hammered out . . . only it was discovered afterwards that a very expensive watch in the purse of one of her sisters-in-law went missing—which my patient had nicked when the woman had gone to the ladies' room. That was the last straw. After that, her father arranged for her to live with his sister in a different city, agreeing to give her a modest sum monthly for the support of his grandchild, but nothing further, and breaking off all further contact. One of the reasons for the failure of this treatment effort was the inability of the patient to avail herself of what I have, only partly in jest, called "Stone's Rule." According to Stone's Rule, no one on welfare or who receives, as she did, a certain sum from an ex-lover, will be motivated to work—as I and all her family urged her to do—unless she could earn at least 1.5 *times as much* working as she could by living off the system. Why work for a thousand dollars a month if the government or someone else is giving you a thousand dollars a month? A job making fifteen hundred or two thousand a month would make enough of a difference in one's life to warrant the effort. But she had no skills that could qualify her for a job that met this criterion. So she continued her parasitic way of life.

Case 3

A woman of twenty-four, who had just graduated law school, was referred to me by a boyfriend she had met through the Internet. He was twice her age and was looking for someone to marry and have a child with. She was looking for a "sugar-daddy" to help her out financially till she was self-sufficient. They lived in different states and seldom had the chance to be together, though they communicated frequently by phone and e-mail. As she revealed to him in the course of these communications, she had grown up in a family where the parents had divorced when she was seven—after which her father was allowed to visit only under supervision for some length of time. His brother carried on a continual incestuous relationship with her— with threats to kill her if she told anyone. Her brother and mother are supposedly unaware of this even to this day. She mentioned to her boyfriend that her father also had molested her sexually—but then again she would deny that and say "no, it never happened." At various times she would say the incest with the uncle was still going on; at other times, she would deny this. In a like vein she would tell her cyber-boyfriend that she wasn't seeing any other men, but then the next day would reveal to him that she had lied to him—and that she had met a man via the Internet and had had sex with him, saying—"because I am lonely." In her first dream that she told me *"there were spiders, that, every time I would turn on the light, would be everywhere.* I'm deathly afraid of spiders . . . creepy, they sneak up on you . . . there had been one on the ceiling the night before and I was afraid it'd walk all over me." I have heard many such dreams over the years—with insects and spiders—that allude to incestuous incidents or early incest-like experiences or fantasies; even the word insect is close to incest, and conveys the sense of something unpleasant invading one's body. She did not make any such associations. In a subsequent dream: "I get in a car with a guy . . . he touched me and I felt paralyzed; I couldn't stop him." By this time she had pretty much broken up with the older man—and had become sexually involved with a still older man, a divorcé, who claimed to have had an incestuous relationship with his daughter, and who liked to have "daddy-daughter" sex with younger women. They too met via the Internet, only he lived in the same city as she. He insisted she call him "Daddy" and he called her his "daughter." This literally reduplicated the original incest experiences, granted that she never told me flat out that her father molested her a few years before her uncle began to. She would at times hint at this, at other times, deny, at still other times, hem and haw, refusing to discuss the issue openly. Once ensconced in the Daddy-Daughter affair with the new man, she broke off treatment, saying she couldn't afford it. The first older man had been paying for her sessions; in retrospect, it seems she was using him as a financial cushion, but also as a kind of asexual, good father (as she had never had before), with whom sex was as off limits as it is supposed to be with one's father—while she then took up with the new sexual-father, reliving the past with which she was familiar. The incest with the uncle lasted throughout her adolescence, as far as I could determine, and perhaps even into her 20s. As a result of her sordid background, she felt she didn't belong among ordinary people and could never be satisfied with conventional life. Her lying, withholding, and coyness all combined to keep her immured in the old familiar pattern, since by not talking about it openly, there was no way to begin to make her peace with it, put it into the past, and move on to more socially acceptable relationships.

Antisocial Personality Disorder

Since DSM-IV requires only three of the seven items under Antisocial Personality Disorder, even someone with no more than deceitfulness (as indicated by repeated lying . . .), irritability/aggressiveness, and lack of remorse—can fit under this rubric. Some years ago I treated a woman in her 30s who came from a family with a fair number of first-degree bipolar relatives. She had been hired and fired from a number of jobs, owing to the way her hostile disposition and irritability alienated her from both coworkers and superiors. Her parents, who lived in a different state, were paying for her therapy. Shortly after we began our work, she chanced to visit them for a holiday. She got into a rage at her parents over some trivial incident. Upon her return, she received an envelope with photos she had taken of her relatives while there. She showed me a picture of her parents—in which she had taken an E-Xacto knife and cut out their eyes. She proudly announced to me that she was going to send it to them, as a way of "getting back at them." I suggested to her that it would be much better if she and I talked about the feelings that had moved her to do this, rather than to send the enucleated photo, since that might well infuriate them—to the point of cutting off her treatment. She said she would think about it. Three days later I received a call from her mother. I told her "I know why you're calling!" and described to her how I had tried, obviously unsuccessfully, to head trouble off at the pass. Her mother recounted to me various other incidents when her daughter had behaved in a similarly belligerent and contemptuous fashion. Remarkably, she had a boyfriend at this time—a very gentlemanly and passive young attorney, as I later came to learn—toward whom she was extremely controlling and demeaning. She criticized all his friends, and set about alienating him from them—many of whom told him they couldn't stand her and that he had to choose between her and this or that friend. He slavishly went along with her. She criticized even the way he walked across a street, as though he ought to have started with the right rather than the left foot, and so forth. He invited her, nevertheless, to his family for Thanksgiving, where they were to announce their engagement. When all were seated, she told the gathering: "Tom (as I shall call him) gave me herpes, and so he has to marry me, and Dr. Stone agreed with this!" In point of fact, she had given him herpes, and I of course had never endorsed such an outrageous action in the first place. I insisted on meeting with both of them, which gave me the opportunity to confront her about her lie, and its viciousness, with him present. I then dismissed her from treatment—the first of only two times I have done that since I was in practice. I then began working with him. He had been so beaten down, it took some months before he could extricate himself from this disastrous relationship. She stalked him for a while; he caught her peering into the keyhole of his apartment a few times—which helped convince him that she was not the woman he wanted to spend the next fifty years of his life with. A year later he met a lovely and decent woman, and married her. It is written in the Talmud Sanhedrin that *To save one person is to save the World.* I cannot say that I have saved the world, by the look of it, but I did at least save this one man.

Psychopathy Without Violence

In making a diagnosis of psychopathy one currently relies mostly on the criteria set forth by Robert Hare and his colleagues in Vancouver. They use a 20-item scale, broken down into two main factors: Factor-I, emphasizing severe narcissistic and also some emotional attributes; and Factor-II, devoted to behavioral qualities. The checklist is criminalogically oriented, having been developed mostly from work with prisoners and forensically hospitalized offenders. For me—the essence of the psychopath is the extreme narcissism, as encapsulated in the items: glibness and superficial charm, grandiosity, deceitfulness/lying, manipulativeness/exploitativeness, callousness, absence of remorse, shallow affect, and inability to take responsibility for ones actions. Some of the behavioral items: impulsivity, poor behavioral controls, need for stimulation . . . can change for the better over the years. The personality traits remain fixed. One sees persons exhibiting predominantly the Factor-I aspects of psychopathy mostly in the higher social classes. Their families have been able (often with the generous help of their own "superego lacunae") to bail out or bribe the authorities to go light on adolescents (or young adults) who get into trouble. The behavioral irregularities may be present, but no arrests or convictions result—so the Psychopathy Checklist scores end up below the level where a definite diagnosis is made. Hare sometimes speaks of such people as white-collar psychopaths.

Case 4

One such person that I had attempted to treat was a woman of forty with two small daughters. She came from a wealthy real estate family where her brothers were now in charge. They took care of her needs via a trust. She had been married to a man who had apparently died of a heroin overdose, though there was the nagging question as to whether she had murdered him by giving him an extra-large dose. The neurologist who referred her to me thought that was the case, but nothing was ever proven, since the husband was quite capable of dying by misadventure just on his own. I was never able to resolve that question. She herself was a cocaine addict, and added to her income from trust and inheritance—by dealing. Though referred to me for "depression," I saw no signs of it; if anything she was usually glib, overly cheerful, and bouncy. I noticed that she would often excuse herself to go to the bathroom, always taking her purse, and always emerging happier than she had entered it. It gave new meaning to the expression "powder room." She denied snorting cocaine in the bathroom, even though she once showed me a little jewel-box in her purse where she kept some of the white powder. I insisted she get tested for cocaine, to which she reluctantly agreed. The test came back a few days later positive for ecgonine—which is the metabolite of cocaine. She breezily told me that the benadryl she took for sleep gave "false positives" for ecgonine, but I had already checked this out with my old roommate from medical school, now a professor of pharmacology at a medical school. He assured me that there was a grand total of one chemical that gave a positive test for that substance: cocaine. When I confronted her about the false "false positive"—she became furious. I told her I could not work with her unless she entered a narcotics-anonymous program designed to help with cocaine addiction. She refused—and became the second patient I dismissed from treatment.

Case 5

Another such patient I treated many years ago was a man of twenty-six who needed help finding his place in the world. He had come from a large and prosperous family; his mother had died when he was in his teens; his father was a confirmed alcoholic living off dividends from the family business. His father had given him a new convertible for his high-school graduation—which he "totaled" three days later. But he had inherited several hundred thousand dollars the year before, which he had not as yet managed to go through—so he went and bought a "carbon copy" of the smashed car, parking it in the family garage, with his father none the wiser. He had the Factor-I psychopathic traits of charm, glibness, shallow affect, and deceitfulness, all decked out appropriately in his *Gentleman's Quarterly* façade. He had never worked a day in his life, though he did have many girlfriends—at times several at once. I felt it was crucial to his treatment that he find a job. An uncle in the real estate business came to the rescue, and offered him a position selling commercial buildings. It wasn't more than a month after starting that he regaled me with stories of his startling success—in selling one particular building, for example, that went for a hundred thirty million. After several other such megadeals, I became curious, since—despite my ignorance about the real estate business—it seemed too good to be true for a novice to become such a mover and shaker inside a few weeks on the job. So I got in touch with the family trustee who governed their finances—who informed me that my patient really only sat with his feet on the desk at his uncle's place, reading *Sports Illustrated*. He hadn't sold anything at all, nor earned penny one for the company.

Case 6

The last example of a nonviolent psychopath concerns a woman nearing forty who had just divorced for the fifth time. Her life contained so many examples of lies, deceptions, scams, thefts, frauds, and seductions of judges and prosecutors who had started out to try her for her numerous and varied offenses—as to fill a series of B-movies. A bit weather-beaten when I was asked to evaluate her, she had apparently been something of a beauty in her younger days, using this as capital on which to draw when swindling money from her various swains. She asked one fiancé, masquerading as an heiress whose big monthly check hadn't gotten deposited at the bank yet, if he could lend her $30,000 over the next few weeks. Meantime, she used her seductive charms to seal their whirlwind affair with an engagement ring. They married very soon after, which rendered moot any need to repay the "temporary loan." That was husband number two. Husband number four she snared by a different ruse, telling him shortly after the ceremony that she was pregnant. This time she was too clever by half, as they say: her husband, who had his fill of children by a previous wife, went and had a vasectomy, meaning she was either cheating on him or lying. He found both those possibilities unattractive and divorced her. She did have a child by her fifth husband, but he too quickly divorced her when he caught her trying to divert large sums of money from his business to her private account. A custody battle ensued. During that period, she was arrested for drunk driving and for cocaine possession. She was able to weasel out of those charges, though was put on probation—and went right back to her old habits. But this time, to avoid further arrest, she had her son—teenager from her first marriage!—exchange clothes with her, and driver's licenses—such that the next time she was caught by the police, she managed to pass for her son, and had his valid license. My evaluation of her as an off-the-chart psychopath did at least have the happy result in court of awarding custody to her younger child's worthy and devoted father.

Psychotherapy in a Forensic Patient

When I began working at a forensic hospital twelve years ago, and was in charge of a unit, I admitted a man in his 40s who claimed to be depressed. He had been arrested for drug possession and seemed mentally ill while in the jail, so was sent to our hospital for evaluation and treatment. When he exchanged his clothes for hospital attire, it was noted that he had secreted a wooden knife (a "shiv") in his shoe, which of course raised a red flag, since depressed people don't ordinarily hide weapons about their person. He proceeded to tell me that, although he had been working as a cook, he was now depressed because his wife and two children were all killed in the crossfire during a gangland shoot-out as they were coming out of church in their Virginia coast town. Seven people had been killed altogether in the massacre. Taking a family history, I learned from him that he was "one of fourteen children"—two of whom were named William and Willie, because his mama had run out of names. He gave me many of their names, phone numbers, and addresses. Since I am familiar with investigative work in connection with my follow-up research, I got on the phone to the city where the massacre supposedly took place, and called the newspaper, the mayor's office, and the police bureau—inquiring about a mass murder of seven people occurring in April of 1995. Anyone in that city would have recalled such an incident from the year before—except that there had been none. There were no persons with the names he had given me for his wife and daughters in anyone's files. I then called all the numbers he had recited to me in the Carolinas and in Virginia. Interestingly, all the numbers did indeed correspond to people with the names he mentioned, but they were all white, whereas my patient was black, and none was related to him even by the "six degrees of separation" highlighted in John Guare's 1990 Broadway play (also about a con man). I had to admire my patient for finding all those names in various phone books and memorizing the numbers, even though his story was all a tissue of lies. He was very angry when I confronted him about this, but as a result of his lying, we were able to send him back to jail the very next day—to await his day in court. I have often wondered how it was he imagined that, contrary to Lincoln's admonition, he could fool all of the people all of the time.

Violent Psychopaths

Because of my interest in the extremes of personality disorder, having branched out beyond BPD in the last two decades, I have been asked to serve as expert witness in murder cases where the offender had been called narcissistic, or antisocial, or borderline—the accuracy of which was to be determined by someone knowledgeable in the field. This led in the recent years to my serving as host in a TV program called *Most Evil*, built around my work on what I had called the Gradations of Evil in relation to murder. By way of garnering "live material" for the program, I was sent around the country to interview various serial killers who illustrated different topics relative to the broad domain of murder. One of the programs that aired in 2006 was entitled "Liars." That hour featured Arthur Shawcross, Susan Smith, and David Paul

Brown—alias "Nathaniel Bar Jonah." Each case was horrific in its own way; the circumstances were such as to evoke the label "evil" from the public—in keeping with my contention that the only meaning we can extract from the word evil—is to regard it as an emotional term that people in ordinary life use when an act—usually a violent act—so surpasses human understanding and so shocks our sensibilities that we automatically cringe in horror and disgust, and utter the word "evil." So much for semantics.

The Case of Susan Smith

To begin with the least dreadful, there was the case in South Carolina of the borderline and antisocial woman, Susan Smith, who fell in love with the son of the boss in the place she worked, following her divorce. She had two small boys at the time. Her new lover eventually grew disenchanted with Susan and was about to break off the relationship. Thinking that perhaps unburdening herself of the children would heighten her marriage prospects, she strapped them in the back seat of her car, and drove near a lake, then getting out of the car and pushing it into the lake, drowning her two boys. Savvy enough to grasp the opprobrium with which such an act would be surrounded, were she to admit what she had done, she then saw fit to claim that a black man had commandeered the car and was responsible for the disappearance of her boys, herself miraculously surviving the "kidnap." This is what she said in her interview before the public:

> To everyone who's aware where these two boys are [holding up their pictures], Ah would like to say, *whoevah* has mah children, that they PLEASE bring them home. . . . There's not a minute goes bah, that Ah don't think about those boys, that the Lawd will let them realize that they are missed more than inny children in this world! . . . I want to say to mah babies: your mama loves you SO MUCH . . . Ah've put all mah faith in the Lawd . . . It's such a terr'ble thing to take such children

But then, a few days and a few failed polygraphs later, the truth comes out. There was no black kidnapper. There was only the mother, lying to cover up the planned murder of her two boys (Eftimiades 1995).

Serial Killer Arthur Shawcross

Shawcross had sexually molested a boy and a girl when he was a young man living in Watertown, New York (Norris, 1992). After his arrest, he spent fourteen years in Greenhaven prison as a sexual offender and murderer—until he was unaccountably and unwisely granted a pardon by then governor Cuomo. In his odyssey through New York State afterwards, being kicked out of various cities, he ended up in Rochester, where he embarked on a career of strangling prostitutes—at least eleven that we know of. When I interviewed him in his new abode in the Sullivan County prison, he struck me as having a kind of pseudologia fantastica, since his stories were so Bunyanesque and bizarre. He glorified his past by telling me of his heroic deeds during his service in Vietnam. He spoke of going up in the hills one morning—so high "I could stick my fingers through a cloud" whereupon he then noticed a mama-san with a grenade belt around her waist: "I shot her with my rifle and then cut off her head, nailing it to a tree, to warn the others." Now I knew his history very well, including the fact that he never saw active duty. As for the women he murdered, he claimed to have cannibalized some of them. There was no convincing evidence for this. I twitted him, mentioning "people say when they eat something they're unfamiliar with, that it tastes just like chicken." "Actually," Shawcross told me," "it tastes more like roast pork." Shawcross, for all his crimes, is a jovial man and an artless liar. You can't help liking him, and you can't help being glad he's in prison for life.

David Paul Brown, Another Serial Killer

Brown is a different kind of person altogether. Having grown up in Massachusetts, he was a loner and a misfit all his life (Davidson 2006). He committed his first murder when he was still a child. By his teens his personality had gelled around the attributes of homosexuality and pedophilia. He would dress up in a policeman's uniform and at one point abducted two young boys as they came out of a movie. He tried to sodomize and kill them, but one played dead and was able later to run to the police. He was put in Bridgewater prison where the Boston Strangler had been—and kept there as a sexual offender for fourteen years. He refused all efforts to engage in any form of individual or group therapy. Even so, his mother was able to hire two psychiatrists who convinced a judge that her son was no longer a danger to society. In the meantime he had changed his name to Nathaniel Bar Jonah—so that, as he said at the time, he would know what it was like to experience prejudice for being a Jew. He had been raised in a nonabusive Protestant family. The judge relented and "Bar Jonah" was discharged. A few weeks later he was caught sitting, with all 375 pounds of his bulk, on top of a boy in a car, when his mother was shopping at a mall. When she returned, she screamed and wrestled her son free. When she threatened to press charges, his mother once again came to the rescue, pleading with the woman not to press charges—with the promise that he would be sent to live with his brother in Montana and never return to Massachusetts. The woman took the bait, and he left for

Montana, living by himself, however. In 1996 he dressed, again impersonating a policeman, in a uniform, carrying a stun-gun, and standing outside a grammar school in Great Falls. He waylaid a ten year-old boy, Zach Ramsay, immobilized him with the stun-gun, dragged him to his apartment, sodomized him, killed him, and ate him—feeding those portions of the boy's flesh that he didn't eat—to neighbors, telling them it was "deer meat." Suspected because of his past record as a sexual predator, he was arrested. But there was no body, and the boy's mother was so distraught that she could not accept that her son was dead—so she refused to testify against Bar Jonah. He was sent to prison for other kidnaps—for 130 years without parole, but did not face a murder charge.

When I interviewed him in 2006, he denied the crime entirely, even denying that his apartment, when it was searched, harbored thousands of photographs and pictures of boys, naked and otherwise; he had also written in a code the names of fiendish "recipes" he concocted, such as French Fried Kid, Little Boy Stew, and Wun Yung Boy. But he told me "I'm totally innocent," or "I did no coding." When I asked about the attempted murders back in Massachusetts, he said "I'm not going to get into that. That's long in the past." When I asked him about the bones (of another boy) that were found under his porch, he said "You make it sound like I'm an evil person . . . that wants to do some real harm to people." When asking about why the name-change to "experience prejudice," I asked "why isn't being a homosexual pedophile cannibal enough to earn a measure of prejudice right there?"—he had no answer.

I hope these examples make it clear that lying and deceitfulness are qualities that, like other personality traits, exist on a continuum. They stretch from the treatable—though novel and difficult interventions are often necessary—all the way to the utterly untreatable, as in the last two cases. Susan Smith was ultimately capable of confession and acknowledgement. Those are the first and necessary steps toward ultimate improvement and possible redemption (in the case of serious offenders). Lying and deceitfulness are placed always under the list of qualities associated with antisocial personality or psychopathy, hence they belong to personality configurations that are among the most challenging therapeutically. Beyond a certain point, the cases become untreatable. Psychiatrists don't like to admit that there are untreatable cases (Stone, 2006). It seems almost un-American, as if to say: if we could send a man to the moon, surely we can cure a psychopath, however mendacious and deceitful. As it turns out, it is easier to send a man to the moon.

From an Evolutionary Standpoint

Lying and deceitfulness, though we think of them as negative, undesirable qualities, clearly have their place in the grand scheme not only of human interaction but also of relations in the animal kingdom. Reconsidered in this light, we can say that the clinical and forensic examples above represent lying and deceitfulness carried to such an extreme as to tip the cost/benefit calculus of deceitfulness far to the side of "cost—with very little "benefit."

In the primate world, chimpanzees can be said to have a theory of mind, and show the capacity to lie and deceive when they feel this is advantageous to their welfare. The chimp "Lucy," for example, would lie to her trainer, Roger, after she had defecated in his living room when he wasn't looking: she used the sign language he had taught her to claim that it was not she that did that naughty thing, but rather a graduate student, Sue (Fouts, 1997, p 156). The vervet monkey, likewise endowed with a theory of mind, has special calls of alarm for each predator—if it sees either an eagle, a snake, or a leopard (Maynard-Smith and Szathmáry, 1999, p 143). A clever vervet monkey, banking on this species-wide knowledge, has been known to shout the "eagle" call when it saw a banana on the ground—whereupon all his fellow vervets ran away to flee the "eagle"—leaving the shouter to claim the banana all for himself. Here, benefit outweighed cost. The vervet's ruse would have a counterpart on the human plane, if someone shouted "fire" when there wasn't any—in a hall where people were gathered, so the shouter could take advantage of everyone else's running off—to steal somebody's purse or coat.

Deception can be adaptive, in other words, if the cost/benefit economics are decidedly in the favor of the deceiver (McGuire and Troisi, 1998, p. 139ff). These authors point out that persons will not resort to deception very much, where most people are familiar with one another, as in small towns—since, once caught at any deception, the whole community would be "on" to the deceiver. His chances would be much better if he moved to a different place, or even a different country, where few people knew him, and were thus not in a position to be forewarned about his habit of mendacity and deception. The Scottish forensic psychologist, David Cooke, suggested that the apparent surplus of psychopaths in the U.S. may have stemmed from a significant proportion of crooks and swindlers in Europe, having been spotted as ne'er-do-wells in their native villages in the Old Country, who then decided to strike out for the greener pastures of America, where these persons were not at all known by the local inhabitants, and could thus "con" them the more easily (1998, p. 32). From an evolutionary point of view, what matters is "fitness"—which is the measure of how many offspring an individual leaves to the next generation. In situations where deception works in favor of achieving this biological goal, it can be said to have an advantage, even in cases where someone may have personality characteristics that the community considers undesirable. Thus the clever sweet-talker who cons a woman into marrying him, or at least into sharing her sexual favors with him, may abandon a child they have together, soon after the child's birth. He has thereby gained a notch in "fitness" (one more strand of his DNA goes into the next generation), despite the unsavory reputation he garners by the more honorable (i.e., altruistic, nondeceptive) citizens in the community. Whereas mild and infrequent instances of lying and deception are part of ordinary human experience, we do not bestow negative or "diagnostic" labels on lying and deceptiveness unless they pass beyond a certain socially determined boundary line. When this line is crossed, we are apt to hear of certain "conditions" like: pseudologia fantastica, factitious illness, malingering, compensation neurosis (where a person affects to be more ill than he really is, in hopes of winning a lucrative law suit), and of course, antisocial personality and psychopathy (where conning and manipulativenss are part of the core diagnostic features). McGuire and Troisi are in accord with my view that chronically deceptive persons are difficult (or impossible) to treat, unless therapy can teach them more successful strategies for living that do not involve deceiving others. This is seldom a manageable task. The task is made all the more difficult because therapists, who tend to belong to the nondeceptive world, do not take kindly to being conned and to having the trust between therapist and patient violated. One may speak of a *countertransference* reaction that typically arises in such situations—magnifying further the difficulties in effecting a positive outcome in treatment.

In the forensic domain, there are certain categories of crime where lying and deception are nearly universal. Even psychopathic killers are sensible of the social opprobrium attached to murdering one's parents, spouses, or children. Such persons go to great length to sidestep the embarrassment, not to say vilification, they would be subjected to, were they to acknowledge openly having killed a close relative. We saw this was Scott Peterson, who has never confessed to killing his pregnant wife, Laci (Linedecker, 2003). In my study of uxoricide (men who kill a wife), which now numbers 115, 80 percent have never confessed to the murder. This group, consisting of uxoricides about whom a full biography was written, differs from the more impulsive men who, with no attempt to conceal the deed, kill a wife as she is about to divorce and who then give themselves up to the police. Those men one reads about in the tabloids; they do not engender the interest that warrants a whole book.

But among the 115 in my series, fifty (43 percent) had engaged in "staging"—by which is meant, using various means to make the crime appear accidental, or to "disappear" the wife, so the killer can claim she "ran off" and abandoned home and hearth. Another seventeen men (15 percent) hired a "hit-man" to kill the wife, while the husband was far away, and thus able (in his view at least) to assert that some stranger must have invaded the house and killed his wife, perhaps in an armed robbery.

Among the uxoricides, certain crimes are viewed by the public as more despicable than others: killing a wife who has taken a lover is bad enough; killing a wife purely for insurance money is much worse. One recent example concerns a young Florida couple: Justin Barber and his model-pretty wife, April (Butcher, 2008). Justin was a mid-level executive in a large company, but he had grandiose ambitions about making it big—to which end he engaged in the popular, and for most investors, suicidal hobby of "day-trading." He ran up enormous debts, piled on top of still other debts stemming from his desire to impress everyone by owning three houses whose mortgages he could not meet. To ward off the impending climax, Justin began laying careful plans—taking out two insurance policies for $2,000,000 each, with April paying for her policy (of which he was the beneficiary) and he, for his policy. He kept their finances totally separate. Justin also began googling the Internet to see in what parts of the body a person could shoot himself and survive. This was in preparation for the "perfect crime" he was hatching, where he would kill April in a secluded spot, shoot himself—sustaining only minor injuries, and then lie to the police that an "armed stranger" accosted them as they were making love one evening on the beach. After six months of "due diligence" of this sort, the evening arrived, and in the wee hours at a remote spot near Jacksonville, a few days short of their third anniversary, he shot April in the head, killing her with one shot, and put four bullets into himself—in his hands, plus one in an area of the right chest that his Internet research assured him would be nonfatal. To the police, who proved themselves disconcertingly less stupid than Justin had imagined, he became a suspect immediately. As a result, he drew the *Go Directly To Jail, Do Not Collect the Two Million Dollars* card, though in fairness to his cleverness, it did take several years before the detectives could accumulate hard evidence that would hold up in court. He is now serving a life sentence with no hope of parole. His story is but one of dozens concerning men convinced of their ability to carry off the "perfect crime" of wife-murder, whether for reasons of greed, as in the Barber case, or to avoid the demands of fatherhood (as in the Peterson case), or to free oneself up to be with a mistress (Lew Graham: Lewis, 1990).

Men committing serial sexual homicide routinely use lying and deception in order to lure their victims into positions of helplessness, where they are then at the mercy of the killer. Examples are numerous in my series of 145 serial killers who have been the subjects of full-length biographies. To cite just one such example: Ted Bundy (Michaud and Aynesworth, 1987) would sometimes place one arm in a sling, affecting helplessness, as he "struggled" to carry a bag of groceries from a shop in a mall. Asking a woman if she wouldn't mind helping him place the bag in his car, he would then—as she sat for the moment in the passenger seat, placing the bag in the car—nap the door shut and locked, drive off to an out-of-the-way spot, where he would proceed to rape and kill her.

In evolutionary psychiatry much emphasis is placed on the concept of Resource Holding Power [RHP] (Stevens and Price, 2000). This concept relates to the competition throughout the animal kingdom (and most assuredly within our own ranks) designed to determine who succeeds in obtaining and retaining the resources (food, material goods, and in our case, money) that will insure success in winning and holding on to the most desirable mates by which to parent the most numerous and most successful offspring. Varying degrees of lying and deceptiveness are part and parcel of the games humans play to achieve the greatest RHP. Few of us manage to go a lifetime without resorting to techniques of this sort by way of maximizing our success. Women with the help of "feminine wiles" plus the contributions of the cosmetic industry strive to convince "high-RHP" men of their allure and desirability—by way of increasing the likelihood that they will thus be in a better position to create the best children and, via securing the attachment of the high-RHP father, to provide for the health and welfare of her offspring until they can be launched safely and successfully into the adult world. Men with their prowess and ambitions, helped in many instances by boasting of having graduated from prestigious colleges they never really attended, or of having outrun or outscored various male rivals, hope to attract the women with the most beauty (which usually equates with physical health), sexiness, and steadfastness—so that his children will have the best mothers and the best chances of carrying his genes into the next generation. Provided our tales are not too tall, and our deceptions not too glaring, all this gamesmanship is tolerated, even encouraged. This is lying and deceitfulness that remains "within acceptable bounds." This chapter reminds us how far out of bounds some of us are willing to go in order to gain an unfair quantity of resource holding power. From the perspective of treatability, when faced with lying and deceitfulness that transgresses acceptable bounds, there are two broad areas: those persons who are still amenable to therapy, still able to ac-knowledge their dishonesty—and who are motivated to improve their life-strategies so as to be less reliant on offensive degrees of these undesirable propensities. But then we must recognize that there are some persons, in-cluding a few who are referred to us for treatment, who belong to the area that is totally out-of-bounds—where lying and deceitfulness so dominate the clinical picture and so often prove themselves to be the accompaniments of dangerous activities—that incarceration may have to take the place of treat-ment. In such cases the needs of the public and its safety supercede those of the persons in question.

References

Aichhorn, A. (1925). *Verwahrloste Jugend: Die Psychoanalyse in die Fürsorgeerziehung.* Leipzig: Internationale Psychoanalytische Bibliothek XIX.

Butcher, L. (2008). *To Love, Honor, and Kill.* New York: Pinnacle Books.

Cleckley, H.M. (1941). *The Mask of Sanity.* St. Louis: C.V. Mosby.

Cooke D.J. (1998). Psychopathy across cultures. In: *Psychopathy: Theory, Research and Implications for Society.* eds., D.J. Cooke, A.E. Forth & R.D. Hare, pp. 21–37. Dorderecht,The Netherlands: Kluwer.

Davidson, P. (2006). *Death by Cannibal.* New York: Berkley Books.

Deutsch, H. (1955). The imposter: contribution to the ego psychology of a type of psychopath. *Psychoanalytic Quarterly* 24: 483–505.

Eftimiades, M. (1995). *Sins of the Mother.* New York: St. Martin's Press.

Fouts, R. (1997). *Next of Kin: My Conversations withy Chimpanzees.* New York: Avon Books.

Kraepelin, E. (1909–1915). *Psychiatrie 8th edition,* 4 volumes. Leipzig: J.A. Barth.

Lewis, C. (1990). *Blood Evidence.* Little Rock, AR: August House.

Linedecker, C. (2003). *The Murder of Laci Peterson.* New York: America Media Inc.

Maynard-Smith, J. and Szathmárty, E. (1999). *The Origins of Life: From the Birth of Life to the Origins of Language.* Oxford, UK: Oxford University Press.

McGuire, M. and Troisi, A. (1998). *Darwinian Psychiatry.* New York: Oxford University Press.

Michaud, S.C. and Aynesworth, H. (1987). *The Only Living Witness.* New York: Simon & Schuster.

Norris, J. (1992). *Arthur Shawcross: The Genesee River Killer.* New York: Windsor Publications.

Prichard, J.C. (1835). *A Treatise on Insanity and Other Disorders Affecting the Mind.* London: Sherwood, Gilbert & Piper.

Schmideberg, M. (1959a). Psychiatric treatment of the female offender. *Correction* 24: 7–8.

Schmideberg, M. (1959b). Psychiatric treatment of juvenile delinquents. In: *Symposium on Child and Juvenile Dynamics*, ed. B. Karpman, pp. 240–245. Washington, DC: Psychodynamic Series.

Stevens, A. and Price, J. (2000). *Evolutionary Psychiatry: A New Beginning*, 2nd Edition. London: Routledge.

Stone, M.H. (2006). *Personality Disorders Treatable and Untreatable*. Washington, DC: American Psychiatric Press.

CHAPTER SEVEN

~

Lies and Their Deception

Clarence Watson, J.D., M.D.

All other swindlers upon earth are nothing to the self-swindlers, and
with such pretences did I cheat myself. Surely a curious thing. That I
should innocently take a bad half-crown of somebody else's manufacture,
is reasonable enough; but that I should knowingly reckon the spurious
coin of my own make, as good money!

Charles Dickens, *Great Expectations*

Lies, fibs, prevarication, deception—these terms connote, in varying degrees,
the purposeful distortion of the truth. As has been noted, such distortions are
commonplace in our society, and to some extent, may frequently serve to facilitate everyday interpersonal interactions (Ford, 1999). Individuals, who
are recognized for their mastery of social "tactfulness," utilize to some degree
the ability to *at least* minimize the impact that full candor may produce. After all, in certain situations the saying, "too much of a good thing," that is,
too much of the truth, may be apt.

It has also been noted that the ability to deliberately communicate "untruth" represents an important developmental milestone in children (Ford et
al., 1988). Clearly, in order to lie, one must first possess the concept of what
is the truth and then intentionally deviate from that truth. A child's increasing understanding of the distinction between reality and fantasy and his
growing ability to manipulate this distinction are important components of
the normal developmental process. A child practices the manipulation of
this distinction as he discovers that his mother cannot read his mind and

searches for a boundary limit between himself and mother; and later, in adolescence, as a means to protect his autonomy, which the adolescent perceives to be under siege by intrusive parental figures, during his quest for a self-determined identity (Goldberg, 1973).

Besides the distortions of truth that manifest during normal cognitive development or those which are elements of the practice of social "tactfulness," there are those distortions that are considered morally unacceptable or behaviorally abnormal. In this vein, one must also consider that such distortions are not simply isolated to interpersonal exchanges between individuals, but may also be expressed internally in the form of self-deception. The capacity and practice of lying to one's self may, as with external lies to others, range from the benign to the malignant; the norm to the pathological.

It is within this context that Dr. Michael Stone addresses the interplay of personality and deception in his paper, *Lying and Deceitfulness in Personality Disorders*. Dr. Stone sets the foundation of his paper by defining the terms "lying" and "deceitfulness." He explained that, while "lying" involves the deliberate and fully conscious intention of *telling* something that is untrue; deceitfulness, on the other hand, refers to *any* effort to twist facts or mislead others from the truth. Dr. Stone's explanation underscores the idea that all lies involve deception, but that deception may not always involve lies. For example, the act of withholding the truth in some situations may be considered deceitful, and thereby, a form of deception; but on its own, this act may not possess the necessary elements of an untrue statement that would represent a lie.

Dr. Stone further distinguishes customary exaggerations and minimizations that are symptomatic of psychological resistances held by ordinary psychoanalytic patients from the "purposeful lack of candor" involved in lying and deceitfulness. In his view, it is uncommon to encounter among better functioning patients in psychoanalysis much more than these exaggerations and minimizations. Despite this distinction, it should be noted that just as exaggerations and minimizations may defend against embarrassment and shame, lying and deceitfulness often operate in the same way. As such, under certain circumstances, the line of demarcation between exaggerations and minimizations and lying and deceitfulness is nebulous; as each, one could argue, are forms of deception. Additionally, this distinction does not directly address the concept of self-deception upon which these minimizations and exaggerations may be based. While self-deception may serve a protective function for self-esteem utilizing minimizations and exaggerations, it may also employ the frank deceitfulness and lying seen in particular personality disorders.

In keeping with his distinction, Dr. Stone identifies two broad groups that, throughout his experience, regularly engaged in lying and deceitfulness. The first group includes borderline, antisocial, and psychopathic patients. The other group arose from Dr. Stone's forensic experience with mentally-ill offenders and violent prisoners. Throughout his paper, Dr. Stone provides rich case examples from these groups and illustrates a continuum of deceitfulness practiced by individuals with personality disorders. Briefly, some of the examples are as follows:

- A high school student diagnosed with borderline personality organization with narcissistic traits reported to his psychoanalyst that he was "creaming" his academic courses, when in reality he was failing the coursework and hardly attending school.

- A woman, diagnosed with borderline personality disorder, who fixated on the spouse of her psychiatrist and regularly spread malicious rumors about female coworkers.

- A woman diagnosed with antisocial personality who falsely announced to her family that her fiancé had to marry her because he gave her a sexually transmitted disease when, in fact, she had infected him. She also falsely claimed that her psychoanalyst, Dr. Stone, was in agreement with this false statement.

- The highly publicized case of Susan Smith, who intentionally drove her car into a lake, drowning her two sons who were passengers. She lied to police and the public, stating that an African American man had stolen her car and abducted her children.

- David Paul Brown, a sexual sadistic serial killer, who abducted child victims using ploys such as impersonating a police officer. He also fed neighbors the remains of one of his victims, claiming that it was "deer meat."

When reading Dr. Stone's examples, one is compelled to examine the characteristics of the lies involved in each case. While the examples provide vivid descriptions outlining particular instances of lies and deceitfulness, the reader is left wondering about the underpinnings of deception in these cases and in personality disorders generally. The following questions could be asked: What are the intrapsychic dynamics in personality disorders that support the seemingly apparent external motivations to lie? Are there specific types of lies and deception that certain personality disorders characteristically

utilize? Do these lies represent treatable symptoms of an underlying personality disorder or are they essential for the protection of a brittle core personality? The significance of these questions have special relevance when deceptive practices repeatedly impact the deceiver's interpersonal
relationships, occupation and, in forensic settings, personal liberty interests.

Lies and Deception

Perhaps, as a starting point, the overall nature of lying should be reflected
upon. Most definitions regarding lying state, more or less, that it is the expression of untruth with the intent to deceive. There is some debate as to
whether a lie requires an explicit communication from one person to another
or whether simply withholding the truth falls within the definition. In other
words, does omission of the truth always count as a lie? Regardless of one's
view on this issue, it is clear that explicit lies, along with deliberate omissions
of truth, fall within the larger category of deception. Deception, itself, has
been defined as the intentional setting up of circumstances in order that another person will not possess sufficient knowledge of the reality of the situation to allow him successfully to pursue his goal (Bursten, 1973, p. 74). Such
intentional distortions of the truth are often aimed at influencing the
thoughts and actions of another who may think or act differently if the reality of the situation had been known to them; thereby, offering the deceiver
means to satisfy his disguised conscious or unconscious goals to the detriment
of the deceived.

Unquestionably, there are instances when the deceiver and the deceived
are one in the same. Self-deception may be the end product of various unconscious psychological defenses operating to protect the ego. Self-deception
may also result when an individual habitually reports a lie consciously, but
over time comes to believe the lie to be true; much like, taking the "spurious
coin" of one's own make as good money as in Dickens' novel, *Great Expectations*. In this way, such self-deception can contribute to the conception and
preservation of one's "personal myth" (Kris, 1956).

As previously stated, certain types of misrepresentations of the truth may
be considered socially acceptable. Sparing the feelings of a loved one who has
given a gift that does not meet one's tastes may fall into this category. Further, as Dr. Stone discusses, there may even be an evolutionary benefit to the
ability to distort the truth. But, what appears critical to whether a lie is considered socially acceptable or not depends on the circumstances, motivations, and extent of the lie. Generally, some common motivations for lying
include lies to avoid punishment, to avoid shame and maintain self-esteem,

to protect another person, and to manipulate another for material gain or to inflict physical harm. Other types of lies that have been outlined include lies to preserve autonomy, lies as an act of aggression, lies to obtain a sense of power, lies for the delight of putting one over, lies as wish fulfillment, lies to maintain self-deception, and lies to create a sense of identity (Ford, 1999, pp. 87–102). Remarkably, there are individuals who regularly engage in lies that do not appear to have any motivation and fit the description of pathological liars (Dike et al., 2005).

There is also the curious occurrence of individuals who purposefully lie to their own detriment. Examples of this include unsolicited voluntary false confessions to crimes given in the absence of external coercion by law enforcement (Kassin, 1997). Take, for example, the hundreds of individuals falsely confessing to the 1932 kidnapping and murder of Charles Lindbergh, Jr. (Rogge, 1959) or the more recent case of the false confession to the murder of JonBenét Ramsey (Johnson, 2006). Individuals providing these false confessions may be motivated by a quest for notoriety, guilty feelings about another transgression, or a desire to protect another person (Gudjonsson, 1992). Of course, as pointed out by Dr. Stone, various personality disorders are prone to lying and deceitfulness and the associated motivations for deception are abundant. In the next section, I will attempt to explore further the intersection between these personality disorders and the practice of deception.

The Personality Disorders

Some personality disorders appear to have more of an affinity for lying and deception by their nature. As outlined by Dr. Stone, antisocial and borderline personalities fall within this category. However, other personality disorders, including narcissistic, histrionic, and obsessive compulsive personality disorders have also been recognized for their proclivity for deception (Ford et al., 1988). Whether it is to protect a fragile self-image, to draw others into an idealized relationship, or to set the stage to victimize another person, these lies are manifestations of the significant superego defects underlying these personality disorders. Briefly, lies and deceitfulness used in histrionic personality disorder may relate to creating a dramatic effect, to avoid unpleasantness, or to ingratiate themselves to others (Ford, 1999, p. 115). While the deception commonly utilized by the obsessive compulsive personality is often protective against external control by others (Ford et al., 1988, p. 560). At this point, Dr. Stone's case examples require a more extensive review of the personality disorders outlined.

Borderline Personality Disorder

Dr. Stone covers a number of individuals with the primary diagnosis of borderline personality disorder. Central to these case examples are the tumultuous interpersonal relationships which characterize borderline pathology. Given the nature of the borderline personality, it is no surprise, as Dr. Stone illustrates, that individuals with this disorder are prone to lying and deceitfulness. Manipulative behavior, one of the common features of the borderline personality, often involves the distortion of facts aimed at the persons with whom they have or desire intense personal relationships. Whether through attempts to draw persons into these relationships or to viciously attack another during episodes of the extreme rage associated with perceived abandonment—the borderline personality may use lies and deceitfulness to accomplish these objectives.

Important features of the borderline personality support the frequent use of deception. Central to this disorder is the lack of a coherent self-identity and intense fear of abandonment. As a result of their fragmented sense of self, they constantly rely on others for validation. The borderline personality organization, upon which the disorder is based, leads them to alternate between idealization and devaluation of others, as well as themselves (Kernberg, 1967). As a consequence, perceived acceptance by others produces internal validation of the good self, while perceived rejection by others spawns devaluation of the self and the expectation of abandonment. Accordingly, these individuals are highly sensitive to signs of acceptance or rejection by others. Their propensity towards idealization and devaluation of others, as well as their own internal self-image, consistently leaves the borderline personality at odds with those around them. Hence, the borderline personality may engage in lying and deceitfulness in order to maintain the interpersonal relationships that they cyclically annihilate and attempt to resuscitate in order to avoid abandonment. However, these individuals turn a blind eye to the reality that the repetitive deception used to manipulate these relationships may ultimately bring about the destruction of the relationship and the actual abandonment they sought to avoid.

Another important feature of the borderline personality that influences the use of lies and deceitfulness is the impulsive nature of the disorder. These individuals have a diminished capacity for inner restraint on behavior which centers on shame, fear, and a paranoid dread of exposure (Akhtar, 1995). Furthermore, they have such poor impulse control that they may not consider the impact of their words before they speak. In the moment, their desired objective, whatever it may be, takes such precedence over speaking the truth or behaving honestly that the potential consequences of their conduct are reduced to shadowy details. However, even if these individuals were capable of considering those consequences, this may be of little worth, since the borderline personality's proclivity for lying and deception is bolstered by a weak capacity for genuine guilt (Akhtar, 1995).

One must not overlook the chronic vengeful anger simmering beneath this personality's exterior shell which erupts into overt rage with stress. This persistent anger may result in the aggressive use of lies, where hateful rumors are used as weapons to manipulate interpersonal interactions. Additionally, the borderline personality may use fantasy in an effort to soothe poor self-esteem and communicate their fantasy as real to others in order to accentuate this effect (Ford, 1999). This mechanism may explain to some degree the phenomenon of pseudologia fantastica in borderline individuals (Snyder, 1986).

Dr. Stone's example of the borderline woman, whose deceitfulness included telephone calls to her doctor's home when he was out of town and hanging up upon hearing his wife's voice, nicely illustrates many of the foregoing points. This woman's deceitfulness related to her persistent struggle with the fear of abandonment by her doctor in favor of his wife; that the doctor would dismiss the patient's existence if his wife accompanied him out of town. Further, the volatility of this patient's interpersonal functioning and tendency to devalue others supported her aggressive use of lies, as she regularly initiated vicious rumors about her female coworkers. Moreover, her repeated behavior in this regard exemplified an inadequate capacity for genuine guilt as found in borderline patients.

Antisocial Personality Disorder and Psychopathy

Of all the personality disorders, the antisocial personality is the one in which lying and deceitfulness is incorporated within its definition (American Psychiatric Association, 2000). There has been some ambiguity in the literature as to whether antisocial personality disorder is synonymous with psychopathy or is something less malignant. Some authors use the terms interchangeably (Simon, 1995). Others feel that the definition of antisocial personality disorder is too narrow to fully capture the essence of the psychopath (Meloy, 2004). As outlined by Dr. Stone, while the DSM–IV lists criteria that in varying combinations amount to antisocial personality disorder, separate criteria have been developed for the diagnosis of psychopathy stemming from research with prisoners and forensically hospitalized offenders.

In his paper, Dr. Stone places these terms into separate categories without explicitly elucidating this division, except to say that extreme narcissism is the essence of the psychopath. However, some would argue that extreme narcissism is the essence of antisocial personality, as well; the distinction between narcissistic personality disorder and antisocial personality disorder being that, among other things, the former has more capacity for remorse and the latter has more severe superego pathology (Kernberg, 1992). Conversely, I agree with the view taken by Simon (1995, p. 27) that antisocial personality disorder is the official term for psychopathy and that there are passive and aggressive forms of psychopathy. A review of the literature by Akhtar (2004, p. 245) supports the view of passive and aggressive subtypes within antisocial personality disorder. The passive subtype is parasitic, exploitative of others, and engages in petty swindling; not serious criminal behavior. The aggressive subtype engages in major criminal activities and violence. The major distinction is the quality and degree of the involved antisocial behaviors. Even within these subtypes, one would expect to see variations in degree of pathology in individuals from the mild to the severe. Certainly, the serial killers and sexual sadistic murderers described by Dr. Stone as psychopaths fall within the severe aggressive type.

Prior to the development of the DSM-IV criteria for the diagnosis of the antisocial personality, Cleckley (1941) described the characteristics of the psychopathic personality. According to Cleckley, elements of this personality include superficial charm and good intelligence; the absence of delusions and other signs of irrational thinking; the absence of nervousness or psychoneurotic manifestations; unreliability; untruthfulness and insincerity; lack of remorse or shame; inadequately motivated antisocial behavior; failure to learn by experience; and pathological egocentricity and incapacity for love. Cleckley also pointed out that these individuals show a total disregard for truth and that the "over-emphasis, obvious glibness, and other traditional signs of the clever liar do not show in his words or in his manner."

But, what is it about the antisocial personality that makes him so prone to lying and deceitfulness? Individuals with antisocial personality disorder have such a severe defect of superego that there is an inability to experience inner guilt, a lack of empathy for others, and a disregard for social mores and law (Akhtar, 1995). As a result, the activity of lying and deception may be carried out as easily as reporting the truth, since the antisocial personality does not experience the anxiety that a guilty conscience would manifest. Hence, lies have no moral significance. Perhaps connected with this, are studies that report that individuals with antisocial personality disorder have hypoactive autonomic nervous response systems (Patrick, 1994). Further, Hare and colleagues (1989) proposed that biologically, these individuals may have poor integration of the factual and emotional components of speech, resulting in diminished emotional significance given to their words. As an overall consequence, they are not prone to experience anxiety even when lying in settings where there is a high risk of detection. Such qualities assist these individuals in becoming effective liars, con men, and imposters.

Of the many lies that the antisocial personality employs some common types can be recognized. They may use lies to avoid punishment for prior antisocial behaviors. These lies, of course, do not reflect the individual's regret for the principle antisocial act, but only represent the desire to avoid the displeasure associated with the punishment for that act. These individuals also engage in lies for the pleasure of "putting something over" on others. As outlined by Meloy (2004, p. 99), successfully "putting something over" produces an experience of contemptuous delight in these individuals. The contemptuous delight stems from the enhancement of grandiosity and temporary resolution of inner feelings of inferiority at the expense of the victim. Bursten (1973) described this intrapsychic process as the purging of the shameful, worthless self object and projection of that self object onto the victim; resulting in exhilaration and the purification of the grandiose self. The ability to fool someone provides the antisocial personality with a fleeting sense of power and control. However, since the antisocial individual suffers perpetual feelings of inferiority within his narcissistic core, these reparative efforts through deception must be continually repeated. An extreme form of these types of lies may be pathologic lying, or pseudologia fantastica (Weston and Dalby, 1991).

Lastly, the lies and deceitfulness for which antisocial personalities are well known are predatory in nature. These lies generally involve manipulating a victim into a more vulnerable position in order to take further advantage of him. The lies, then, are tools used to establish the optimal conditions necessary to carry out further antisocial behaviors. Whether it is for material gain or to inflict physical harm on their victims, the lies of the antisocial personality in this context are merely means to a more sinister end. Regardless of whether these lies represent a means or an end, the acts of the antisocial personality illustrate his contempt and devaluation of others. An extreme example of this is Dr. Stone's description of the sexually sadistic serial killer, David Paul Brown, who impersonated a police officer to entrap his child victims. Another example is the serial killer, Ted Bundy, who entrapped young women by placing his arm in a sling, feigning injury, and abducted the unsuspecting women when they attempted to meet his requests for assistance. The deception used by these killers symbolizes only a sliver of the contempt they have for others. Their immeasurable contempt ultimately culminates in the act of killing, which provides absolute power over the victim and temporarily defends against an internal experience of "utter hopelessness and despair."

This subgroup is particularly adept at deception, as noted by Malmquist (2006), citing the cunning and clever deceitfulness of serial killers who have avoided apprehension for prolonged periods, despite ongoing murderous behavior.

Narcissistic Personality Disorder

While Dr. Stone does not specifically address narcissistic personality disorder, other than a case of borderline personality organization with narcissistic traits, features of the narcissistic personality make it worthwhile to discuss in relation to deception. Careful examination of the narcissistic personality reveals how lies and deceitfulness may operate within the framework of this personality disorder. Individuals with this disorder are known for their extreme self-centeredness, grandiosity, and need for admiration from others. They are preoccupied with attaining tremendous success and are relentless in their search for glory and power (Akhtar, 2004). Kohut (1971) introduced the term, the "grandiose self," upon which these elements are based. Kernberg (1984) contributed to the concept of the "grandiose self," albeit from a different etiological perspective than Kohut.

The grandiosity of the narcissistic personality leaves these individuals intolerant of failures and imperfections in themselves (Nemiah, 1961). However, beneath their grandiose exterior, they are fragile, filled with feelings of inferiority and vulnerable to shame (Akhtar, 2004). Consequently, they experience difficulties in regulating self-esteem and often react to criticism with depression or anger (Ford, 1999). Accordingly, for the good of their self-esteem, individuals with this disorder require the actual or perceived admiration of others.

Why, then, would an individual with narcissistic personality disorder engage in lies and deceitfulness? Surely, such deceptive practices would not engender feelings of admiration in others. Interestingly, these individuals portray themselves as noble and possessing zeal and enthusiasm about moral and sociopolitical matters (Akhtar and Thompson, 1982). Covertly, however, they possess a corruptible conscious and a readiness for the shifting of their values (Akhtar, 2004). Such shifting in values may result from the confluence of their sense of entitlement, as their self-perceived uniqueness places them above the rules, and their enduring pursuit of power. As a result, they may consider their mendacity as justified means for attaining their lofty goals. Further, since they generally consider others as beneath them, there is little consideration given to the impact of deception on others, especially when the fulfillment of their grandiose aspirations is within reach. This quality is buttressed by the narcissist's lack of empathy for others. Overall, their frank manipulation of others may be part of a "by hook or by crook" mentality to accomplish their goals.

Just as critical to the narcissistic personality is the protection of a vulnerable self-esteem. Grandiosity, as discussed previously, operates to protect that self-esteem. These efforts at protecting self-esteem utilize self-deception along with the active deception of others. In fact, a measure of self-deception, in this regard, is necessary for the narcissist to defend against a depressive state that could arise in the absence of a grandiose self-concept. Despite the reality of their personal situation, the narcissistic personality may lie to others in order to appear in closer proximity to their internal idealized grandiose self. They may lie to avoid the shame and embarrassment that exposure of their actual station in life may bring, since, they must always appear in the most positive light. As concisely noted by Akhtar (2004, p. 69), the narcissistic personality has a tendency to change the meaning of reality when facing a threat to self-esteem. Such tendencies may result in distortions of the truth when communicated to others.

Detecting Deception

Unlike the beloved protagonist of Collodi's 1883 literary classic, *The Adventures of Pinocchio*, the overwhelming majority of individuals do not exhibit such apparent signs of deceptive intent as those suffered by the mischievous wooden puppet. In fact, it is the very lack of obvious indicators of deception and an innate desire to not be deceived that have fueled the ageless quest to detect mendacity. Accordingly, there is great societal interest in identifying liars who would otherwise reap the benefits of undetected deception.

Behavioral Observation

Numerous methods have been employed for the purpose of detecting lies over the course of history. The Chinese once forced criminal suspects to chew rice powder and spit it out; dry powder indicated deception and guilt. The Bedouins of Arabia used red-hot irons to ferret out the truth by forcing suspects to lick the irons; a burnt tongue meant deception. During the Spanish Inquisition, suspects were forced to swallow dry bread and cheese; if it became stuck in the suspect's throat, he was considered a liar. The central premise of these methods relied upon a physiological response associated with increased anxiety; namely, the decreased production of saliva. Hence, it was thought that the inability to produce saliva, as measured by these

rudimentary examinations, ultimately betrayed a liar's intent. Other potential sources of anxiety were often ignored. In that day, beware the innocent
suspect who is fretful that he would not be believed!

Contemporary scholars have searched for the existence of a real life
"growing nose" associated with lying. Ekman and Freisen (1974) proposed
that subtle nonverbal signs in the face and body, referred to as *leakage*, provide clues of deceptive intent. *Leakage* may involve micro-facial expressions, defined as barely perceptible fragments of suppressed expressions that
indicate concealed emotion (Ekman, 2003). These micro-facial expressions
have been considered unconscious physical manifestations that disclose
the intent to deceive. However, Ekman (2003) provides a cautionary re-
mark stressing *Othello's error*, a term that he coined to describe the faulty
presumption that concealed emotion always serves as confirmation of deception. Further, many behaviors commonly associated with deception,
such as shifty eyes or a nervous smile, may simply represent the personal
habits of an individual and nothing more. What has become apparent from
the research to date is that there is no universal *Pinocchio sign* to reliably
detect lies amongst individuals.

Despite the lack of reliable indicators of deceit, people engage in deception detection on a daily basis. Whether in the context of interpersonal or
business relationships, individuals constantly measure the veracity of what
they are being told. There is no other setting where this is more the case than
in the legal arena. Here, the principle purpose is ascertainment of the truth
upon which justice may be served. Indeed, the very nature of the adversarial
process of the courtroom is geared at determining the truth and detecting dishonesty. Through witness testimony, cross-examination, and other evidence,
judges and juries measure the credibility of what is being presented during
trial. This process of determining the truth is especially critical in criminal
cases where a defendant is at risk of losing the liberty of freedom at the very
least, or life at the very most.

Yet, the process of determining the credibility of a criminal defendant begins well before he enters the courtroom. It begins when he has been identified as a "person of interest" during a criminal investigation. The ability to
convey credibility during police questioning will influence whether an individual officially becomes a criminal suspect and, ultimately, a defendant on
trial. Given the significant stakes involved in police investigations, one
would expect that police officers making these determinations would be particularly adept at lie detection. However, one study showed that police officers in general are no better than laypersons at detecting deception (Ekman
and O'Sullivan, 1991). The study further revealed little relationship between

law enforcement officers' *confidence* in their ability to detect lies and their *actual performance* in detecting lies.

It has been shown that the ability to detect lies from demeanor alone is little more than chance (DePaulo et al., 1985). Such factors as personal bias, cultural differences and variations in behavior may contribute to the fallibility of human lie detection. Consequently, techniques purporting to utilize objective measures to detect deception have become particularly appealing. One example, the polygraph, has been used for some time for the detection of lies. Another example, functional magnetic resonance imaging, has received major attention regarding its potential use for detecting lies in the future.

The Polygraph

As previously noted, anxiety has long been associated with the telling of lies. As with the ancient observation that decreased saliva may be a physiological response to the stress of lying, other signs of autonomic arousal have also been identified. The polygraph, developed in the early 1900s, exploits some of these signs. Polygraphs or lie detectors, as they are sometimes called, measure the pulse, blood pressure, respiration, and galvanic skin response of an individual for the purpose of detecting deceit. At the start of a polygraph examination the subject is asked a series of neutral questions for which the answers are already known. These questions establish the subject's physiological response baseline. The subject is then asked more sensitive questions and physiological changes from baseline are noted. Despite the ultimate purpose of the polygraph, it does not actually measure deceitfulness, but at most measures the physiological manifestations of emotional response.

Studies investigating the accuracy of polygraphs have shown a range from 48 percent to 90 percent and an average accuracy rate of 71 percent (Kittay, 2007). The discrepancy in accuracy rates has been associated with variations in examination methods and polygraph examiner expertise, as well as variations in research design. Nonetheless, critics point to these studies to buttress arguments asserting the unreliability of the polygraph. Kittay (2007) noted the National Research Council's statement that polygraph "evidence was scanty and scientifically weak" because, in part, the measured physiological responses are not uniquely associated with deception.

It should be of little surprise, then, that the judicial system in the United States views polygraph evidence with a great deal of skepticism. For the most part, U.S. courts have been unwilling to allow polygraph examinations to be admitted into evidence. The 1923 landmark case of *Frye v. United States* provided the first glimpse of the judicial treatment of polygraph evidence which continues to this day. In that case, a convicted murderer sought to appeal his conviction arguing that the trial court erred in excluding polygraph evidence in his defense. The trial court's decision to exclude the polygraph results was upheld on appeal since the polygraph had not gained general acceptance in the relevant scientific community. As an aside, the significance of the *Frye* decision is not only founded in its treatment of polygraph evidence, but more importantly, it established a major legal standard for the admissibility of all scientific evidence in federal and state courts.

Notwithstanding the potential benefits of a properly conducted polygraph examination, there are major concerns associated with the test. To start, while the test gives the appearance of objectivity, it is, in fact, contaminated by the subjectivity of the polygraph examiner. This represents a major weakness of the polygraph, since the test methodology and interpretation of results may be subject to the biases of the examiner (Underwood, 1995). Another major flaw of the polygraph is that its fundamental method, the measurement of physiological responses, may be influenced by the test subject. Physical and mental countermeasures, such as tongue biting and counting backwards by seven during the neutral question phase, have been effective in *deceiving* the polygraph (Honts and Perry, 1992). Lastly, one must also consider the character of the subject being tested. As previously mentioned, individuals with antisocial personality disorder, who have high proclivity for deception and for whom society has the utmost interest in detecting, have also been shown to possess hypoactive autonomic nervous response systems. Accordingly, the polygraph may have difficulty detecting physiological changes from baseline in these individuals, who do not exhibit the typical manifestations of anxiety associated with deception.

Regardless of the limitations of the polygraph and the judicial treatment of this lie detection technique, the polygraph continues to enjoy widespread use in various settings. For example, while polygraph results are unlikely to be admissible in court, law enforcement routinely uses the polygraph as an investigative tool. In this regard, polygraph tests are used to corroborate witness statements, to eliminate suspects, and to facilitate the interrogation process without the intent to introduce the results at trial (Honts and Perry, 1992). The polygraph is also regularly used by governmental agencies for hiring and security clearance screening.

Functional Magnetic Resonance Imaging

Another instrument that is currently being explored for its use as a lie detection device is functional magnetic resonance imaging (fMRI). The fMRI is an imaging instrument that measures localized brain activity by determining blood flow and oxygen utilization while a subject performs specific tasks. In essence, it allows the specific mapping of brain regions to the subject's correlated observable behaviors. Researchers have attempted to localize areas of the brain associated with lying by scanning a subject while lying and telling the truth. Theoretically, lying requires higher executive functions to suppress truth and as such, is expected to activate brain areas associated with executive functioning (Applebaum, 2007).

While this technique may show some promise in the future, studies have been inconsistent in identifying which brain regions are activated by lying (Applebaum, 2007). One proposed advantage of this method is that it measures actual neural activity and does not interpret physiological responses to emotion (Kittay, 2007). However, a critical point of clarification will need to be addressed; whether, in fact, the presence or absence of emotional response during prevarication impacts fMRI results. Another issue to be considered is whether a partial truth activates the same or different areas of the brain. Further, what of the situation where an individual begins to lie, but ultimately decides to be truthful? The fMRI as a lie detector is wrought with too many questions at this time to merit widespread use. It is likely that, just as the polygraph has been unable to overcome legal obstacles to gain acceptance in the courtroom, the fMRI as a lie detector may befall the same fate.

Concluding Remarks

Dr. Stone's paper illustrates the sweeping disruptive effects that deception in the setting personality disorders may generate in interpersonal and therapeutic relationships. Exploration of the external motivations, intrapsychic dynamics, and ramifications of deceitfulness is critical when treating individuals with personality disorders. Of particular concern is the genuine possibility of countertransference when the therapist becomes the target of their patient's deception. Careful consideration of this issue must be undertaken frankly when deception threatens the therapeutic alliance.

Dr. Stone comments on the range of treatability of lies based on the deceiver's capability for confession and acknowledgment. It should be noted that, while the readiness to confess may sometimes provide a window into the degree of a deceiver's psychopathology, this is not always the case. Depending on the individual, readiness to confess may indicate very little. As with an antisocial personality, who may readily confess under certain circumstances but, by definition, lacks a moral compass and does not experience remorse, the confession may mean nothing more than another effort to manipulate the existing circumstances to his advantage. As such, the confession of a lie alone is not a reliable indicator of treatability. Furthermore, clarification is necessary to determine what we are seeking to treat. Is the readiness of the confession and acknowledgment of a lie an indication that an individual's practice of lying and deceitfulness can be treated? Is it not that chronic deceitfulness represents a symptomatic expression of a core superego defect? We must bear in mind that in the same way a fever due to an underlying malignancy may acutely respond to antipyretics without the readiness of this response predicting successful treatment of the cancer; then too, a lie due to a personality disorder, which is readily confessed in acute response to having been exposed, would not necessarily indicate the probability of successful treatment of the underlying personality disorder. Without more, the fever and the lies could recur. While confession and acknowledgement may be ideal first steps in dealing with chronic deceitfulness, in some personality structures where deceitfulness to others and one's self serves as the glue for a fragile core, such first steps may be precarious. Clearly, the question of treatability in this context is complex, just as the existing literature regarding the treatment of personality disorders suggests.

For psychiatrists and psychologists involved in therapeutic relationships with their patients, the priority of detecting deception may be overborne by more important treatment considerations. In the legal setting, however, forensic psychiatrists and psychologists in the absence of a treatment relationship must include deception detection as an active part of their examinations. During these evaluations, not only is it important to determine the presence of legitimate psychiatric diagnosis, but it is equally important to rule out malingering mental illness. The reason for this becomes apparent when one considers the high stakes involved in legal matters and the obvious motivation to use deception to achieve a particular legal outcome. Despite our best efforts to date, there is no foolproof method to detect deception. In the future, technology may become capable of peering into individuals' minds and uncovering sinister attempts to deceive. But as of today, liars and deceivers may take some comfort in the shelter of fallibility that lie detector technology has yet to overcome.

References

Akhtar, S. (1995). *Quest for Answers: A Primer for Understanding and Treating Severe Personality Disorders*. Northvale, NJ: Jason Aronson.

Akhtar, S. (1992). *Broken Structures, Severe Personality Disorders and Their Treatment*. Lanham, MD: Jason Aronson.

Akhtar, S. and Thomson, J.A. (1982). Overview: narcissistic personality disorder. *American Journal of Psychiatry* 139: 12–20.

American Psychiatric Association (2000). *Diagnostic and Statistical Manual of Mental Disorders (Text Revision) DSM-IV-TR*. Washington, D.C.: American Psychiatric Press.

Appelbaum, P.S. (2007). The new lie detectors: neuroscience, deception, and the courts. *Psychiatric Services* 58: 460–462.

Bursten, B. (1973). *The Manipulator: A Psychoanalytic View*. New Haven, CT: Yale University Press.

Cleckley, H. (1941). *The Mask of Sanity*. St. Louis: C.V. Mosby.

Daniels, C.W. (2003). Part I: using polygraph evidence after Scheffer: the law of polygraph admissibility in American jurisdictions and suggestions for dealing with the recurring legal obstacles. *Champion* 27: 12–39.

DePaulo, B.M., Stone J.I., and Lassiter, G.D. (1985). Deceiving and detecting deceit. In: *The Self and Social Life*, ed. B.R. Sclenker, p. 323–370. New York: McGraw-Hill.

Dike, C.C., Baranoski, M., and Griffith, E.E.H. (2005). Pathological lying revisited. *Journal of the American Academy of Psychiatry and the Law* 33: 342–349.

Ekman, P. and Freisen, W.V. (1974). Detecting deception from the body or face. *Journal of Personality and Social Psychology* 29: 288–298.

Ekman P. and O'Sullivan, M. (1991). Who can catch a liar? *American Psychologist* 46: 913–920.

Ekman, P. (2003). Darwin, deception, and facial expression. *Annals New York Academy of Sciences* 1000: 205–221.

Ford, C.V. (1999). *Lies! Lies! Lies! The Psychology of Deceit*. Washington, D.C.: American Psychiatric Press.

Ford, C.V., King, B.H., and Hollender, M.H. (1988). Lies and liars: psychiatric aspects of prevarication. *American Journal of Psychiatry* 145: 554–562.

Frye v. United States, 293 F. 1013 (D.C. Cir. 1923).

Goldberg, A. (1973). On Telling the Truth. In: *Adolescent Psychiatry: Developmental and Clinical Studies, Vol.*, ed. S.C. Feinstein and P.L. Giovacchini. New York: Basic Books.

Gudjonsson, G. (1992). *The Psychology of Interrogations, Confessions, and Testimony*. Chichester, UK: John Wiley & Sons, 1992.

Hare, R.D., Forth, A.E., Hart, S.D. (1989). The Psychopath as a Prototype for Pathological Lying and Deception. In: *Credibility Assessment*, ed. J.C. Yuille. Dordrecht, Netherlands: Kluwer Academic Publications.

Honts, C.R. and Perry, M.V. (1992). Polygraph admissibility: changes and challenges. *Law and Human Behavior* 16: 357–379.

Johnson, K. (2006). Ramsey case suspect cleared after DNA tests. *The New York Times*, August 29, 2006.

Kassin, S.M. (1997). The psychology of confession evidence. *American Psychologist*, 52: 221–233.

Kernberg, O. (1967). Borderline personality organization. *Journal of the American Psychoanalytic Association* 15: 641–685.

Kernberg, O. (1984). *Severe Personality Disorders: Psychotherapeutic Strategies*. New Haven, CT: Yale University Press

Kernberg, O. (1992). *Aggression in Personality Disorders and Perversions*. New Haven, CT: Yale University Press

Kittay, L. (2007). Admissibility of fMRI lie detection: the cultural bias against "mind reading" devices. *Brooklyn Law Review* 72: 1351–1399.

Kleinmuntz, B. and Szucko, J.J.: (1984). Lie detection in ancient and modern times: a call for contemporary scientific study. *American Psychologist* 39: 766–776.

Kohut, H. (1971). *The Analysis of the Self*. New York: International Universities Press.

Kris, E. (1956). The personal myth: a problem in psychoanalytic technique. *Journal of the American Psychoanalytic Association* 4: 653–681.

Malmquist, C.P. (2006). *Homicide: A Psychiatric Perspective* (2nd Ed.). Washington, D.C.: American Psychiatric Publishing.

Meloy, J.R. (2004). *The Psychopathic Mind*. Lanham, MD: Rowman & Littlefield Publishers.

Nemiah, J.C. (1961). *Foundations of Psychopathology*. New York: Oxford University Press.

Patrick, C.J. (1994). Emotion and psychopathy: startling new insights. *Psychophysiology* 31: 319–330

Rogge, O.J. (1959). *Why Men Confess*. New York: Da Capo Press.

Simon, R.I. (1995). *Bad Men Do What Good Men Dream*. Washington, D.C.: American Psychiatric Press.

Snyder, S. (1986). Pseudologia fantastica in the borderline patient. *American Journal of Psychiatry* 143: 1287–1289.

Underwood, R.H. (1995). Truth verifiers; from the hot iron to the lie detector. *Kentucky Law Journal* 84: 597–642.

Weston, W.A. and Dalby, J.T. (1991). A case of pseudologia fantastica with antisocial personality disorder. *Canadian Journal of Psychiatry* 36: 612–614.

CHAPTER EIGHT

~

Sociocultural Perspectives on Dishonesty and Lying

Daniel M.A. Freeman, M.D.

Pinocchio was 'born' in Italy, but his story[1] is popular in many countries as a symbol of the conflict between truth and lying.[2] In the West, an ideal parent is one who supports and helps a child to not simply be a wooden puppet that conforms to someone else pulling his strings, but rather to become his own real person who thinks, has empathy, and decides. Gepetto was very supportive and encouraged Pinocchio to reach out, explore, and ultimately discover what was true or false in his relationships with others in the world around him. Supported by parental love, Pinocchio progressed from an initial unfeeling and uncaring wooden unresponsiveness, as a self-centered child, to become an understanding real person who preferred right over wrong and felt sad about his own failings (Singletary and Smolen).[3] Maturing in a supportive caring environment, Pinocchio realized that if he lied, it was *his own* nose that grew longer, and his own shame. He repented and ultimately became empathic and caring in his relationships with others

It is easy to assume, within the confines of one's own cultural perspective, that we know what is true and what is false. However different cultures' parameters of truth and of reality vary widely. Each society comes up with its own consensus and formulations regarding some of the most basic questions of life. A culture's judgments and values are shaped by a shared worldview, based upon group members' experiences having grown up in a particular socio-cultural milieu. Beliefs may sometimes be cloaked in absolute certainty as fundamental truths, and they may be worshipped, defended, and mythologized.[4]

Cultural formulations shape the cognitive and affective dimensions of what is considered to be observable or self-evident reality and immutable truth. They provide a springboard for imaginative fictional flights into make-believe. Culture determines which deceptive behaviors or acts are socially acceptable and constructive, and which are to be considered misleading falsehoods that are condemned as lying.[5]

At times we all sidestep the truth and misrepresent certain facts to ourselves and/or to others, both consciously and unconsciously. Internally, we selectively negate and seek to hide dystonic truths, for example when we deny, repress, dissociate, split, project, or idealize. We may alter, reverse, displace, or pretend; and, in so doing, fabricate something entirely new within our inner world of fantasy.

Lying occurs at the interface between the intrapsychic and the interpersonal. In lying, one consciously seeks to mislead others by negating what is real and attributing truth to a pretense or a construct derived from the interplay of primary and secondary processes in one's inner world of illusion and fantasy.

As Dr. Ruth Fischer describes in her chapter, a young child must progress through a number of epigenetic developmental stages (Erikson, 1959) within a supportive milieu, and reach a relatively advanced level of intrapsychic functioning before a full-fledged capacity to knowingly and purposefully mislead and lie becomes possible.

In addition to differences between individual cultures, cultures change, sometimes gradually and sometimes more rapidly. As they change, adult perspectives, the nature of the family milieu and their parenting practices may become modified and reformulated. During the past century, processes of change have accelerated as a result of the communication and transportation revolutions leading mobility and intermingling of people. Children in many cultures grow up in a very different world today than the world of their grandparents. Some of our traditional ideologies, standards, taboos, and prohibitions have loosened or have become modified.[6]

What is truth? Traditionally, we in Western culture have known that it is proscribed to knowingly "bear false witness against thy neighbor" (Exodus 20:16). However, defining the boundaries of lying is complicated in our culture by the fact that we encourage *both* adherence to certain irreducible nonnegotiable rules *and* individuated nonconformity. In seeking to clarify how cultural vantage points are crucial in shaping boundaries between truthfulness and lying, we will compare how this process plays out in our culture with contrasting examples from two other cultures.

Growing Up in One's Family and Culture

In the first year of life, an infant starts to look outward, beyond the intimacy of the symbiotic resonance with mother, trying to contact and explore an enigmatic as-yet-unknown surround.[7] The child tries to grasp and to recognize meaningful patterns and gestalts, begins to differentiate what 'is' or 'is not,' and starts to generate hypotheses concerning what seems to be reliable or untrustworthy.

In the second and third years, culturally-shaped concepts embodied in parental responses, words, and stories contribute to the toddler's efforts to conceptualize, categorize, and respond to the complexities of the outer world. A child tries to figure out and separate what is 'true' from what is 'false.' His efforts to understand and to bridge gaps between contrasting polarities are enriched and continue to evolve in the interplay between his inner transitional symbolic world of imagination and fantasy (Winnicott, 1971), and an outer world of reality, attachments, and interactions.

In their inner world of magical illusion and make-believe, where concerns about truth and reality are temporarily suspended, toddlers try to creatively juxtapose, mould, and shape contrasting images, concepts, and hypotheses. Through pretense and make-believe play enactments, they try out possible solutions. Gradually, with the progressively increasing prominence of secondary process thinking, challenges posed by parental prohibitions, cultural ideals, and the child's need to maintain self-esteem and approval in the eyes of others, contribute to the emergence of superego and ego ideal precursors and subsequent stages of maturation.

There are differences among cultures with regard to what is believed and valued as true or devalued as false. Sometimes expressing the 'whole' truth is culturally unacceptable, and one is *expected* to lie or to consciously conceal what one knows, thinks, or feels. In some instances, pretense and role-playing are culturally acceptable and valued. In others, they are condemned as fraud and inauthentic or as misrepresenting the truth. Sometimes it is deemed culturally essential and constructive for parents to lie to children, in order to protect them or to stimulate and foster what is considered to be their optimal development.

'White lies' are an example of a culturally sanctioned form of lying. People feel that if falsification occurs for a good reason and if it is for the benefit of others, it can be justified or essential, and should not be considered a lie. Sometimes, it is difficult to be both completely honest and simultaneously loyal, considerate, or empathic. Out of consideration for the well-being of a loved one, a member of one's group, or a friend, one may altruistically decide to look the other way, or to falsify or modify the truth. Also, there sometimes are situations when it may be tactful to avoid saying anything about a personally sensitive and/or culturally sensitive topic. One may, in idealization, even lie to oneself about what another person is like, closing one's eyes to their failings. Cultural mores and personal feelings affect these decisions. People often seek a middle ground, attempting to compromise between cultural mores, personal loyalty, compassion, and discretion.

Parents and Children

Parents try to provide a culturally prescribed appropriate environment for their children, including structured experiences, areas of support and reinforcement, puzzling challenges, culturally shared fantasies, opportunities for autonomy, and prohibitions. They may at times encourage children to free themselves from reality and to pretend—either by following the flow of their own fantasies or by dressing up and becoming a cultural hero (such as a princess, a superman, or a pirate). A parent may participate together *with* a child in exploratory make-believe adventures and pretense; or a parent may enact a make-believe role or retell make-believe stories to their child. Dramatized enactments by a parent may be reassuring or sometimes challenging or even threatening.

There may be a cultural mandate for parents to confront their children with challenging, potentially upsetting but growth-promoting scenarios, or alternately with reassuring dramatized enactments or retellings of iconic mythical fantasies. Fictional stories and folktales are presented as though they are true if they are deemed by the group to have potentially protective, didactic, socializing, or growth-enhancing benefits. In Western culture, for example, the characters in such stories range from bogeys and monsters such as the Wicked Witch, Big Bad Wolf, or Devil; to doting grandparental figures like Santa Claus or a Fairy Godmother; or a rescuing hero like a knight in shining armor, or a religious savior.

All cultures establish a balance between hiding and revealing. Parental denial and falsification can be useful in helping children to maintain an inner sense of safety and narcissistic balance until they are old enough for active mastery to become possible. Cultural mores may seek to protectively misrepresent, falsify, or conceal potentially upsetting realities, such as anatomical differences, sexuality, childbirth, and death, in order to prevent the child from possibly becoming traumatized and overwhelmed.

Some Cross-Cultural Comparisons

Western parents have traditionally tried to block a child's early awareness of anatomical differences and sexuality—just as God had done at the beginning of time when Adam and Eve were in the Garden of Eden (Genesis 2:15 to 3:24). Such knowledge could be too traumatic in early childhood when fantasies distorted by unneutralized aggression might become potentially overwhelming. We have felt that it is better initially to be dishonest, to deceive, and to tell children that babies are delivered by a Stork from Heaven. Our pooled wisdom has been that a head-on encounter with reality had best be postponed until a child is ready him or herself to initiate 'eating' from the Tree of Knowledge. Children need to be ready to digest an awareness of sexuality, intercourse, and delivery with relatively more advanced levels of neutralization, self and object constancy, and reality-testing capacities. A child's awareness of many details concerning childbirth and death is similarly postponed, if possible. As long as tentative contacts with awareness of such knowledge evoke overwhelming anxiety (Roiphe and Galenson, 1981), young children often collaborate in maintaining this blindfold of misrepresentation through denial, closing their eyes, not looking, and not letting themselves fully know what they may in fact already partially know. This continues until a more individuated child feels ready to ignore caveats and to start peeking, looking and 'eating the forbidden fruit' in order to understand. The child lets himself 'see' and begins to grapple with the traumatic awareness.

In addition, at some point parents in many cultures feel that it is important that children become able to grapple with essential realities. Therefore, when children seem 'ready' from the vantage point of a particular culture's traditions, parents may start to gradually or more abruptly push the 'young birds' 'out of the nest,' encouraging and stimulating them to try to figure things out. Even at a later stage, letting themselves know what the girl or boy previously hadn't recognized may be upsetting. 'Seeing' nakedness exacerbates oedipal anxieties about castration. Honest frank discussion may be uncomfortable. Conflict may occur if the child 'calls a spade a spade.' Deidealization of the parents may occur when the child starts to discover that 'The Emperor is wearing no clothes!' Adam was so *upset* about losing the shelter of Eden that he tried to project the blame for his own decision to gain knowledge, claiming that it was not his fault because he had been seduced into it by Eve and her evil Serpent! However, removing the blindfold of deception and self-deception serves as a stimulus for a child's increasing use of secondary process thinking to master what initially had seemed incomprehensibly bizarre and intolerably anxiety-provoking.[8]

Western (especially American) parents have traditionally emphasized and tried to encourage their children to become individuated and autonomous as early as possible in their looking, thinking, trying, exploring, and discovering. Although there are limits and requirements for conformity in every culture, and although self-regulation becomes increasingly important as the child grows, a Western parent ideally encourages her child to not simply be a wooden puppet that conforms to someone else pulling the strings, but rather to become an adventurer, confident, and even spunky, as his or her own real person. In infancy, we try to get children to start looking outward and to try to figure things out at the earliest possible stage. Our goal is to establish foundations that will later contribute to their separation, individuation, and autonomy.[9]

We encourage our children to 'speak up' and say what they perceive to be true, telling it 'as it is.' We celebrate iconoclastic initiative and nonconformity, and we like the story of the young boy who spoke up and told the truth that no one else was daring to tell, that "The emperor is wearing no clothes." The Japanese, whom we will be considering below, want their young sons to initially become daring and assertive superheroes (like their mythical heroic super-child Kintaro [or Golden Boy]), but they very abruptly reign in the child's autonomy later. Eskimos, on the other hand, want their children to never become autonomous, but rather to function only within the narrow culturally defined roles that are essential for family survival.

A Western mother does not confine her child to a cradleboard or keep her child skin-to-skin with her in a sling or within her parka, or sleeping in a shared futon. In contrast to mothers in the other cultures that we will be considering, a Western mother puts her infant to sleep in the baby's own cradle or crib, often in a separate room. Traditionally, we sometimes leave our infants and young children in the care of relatives or babysitters, so that the mother can go out to work, have some 'down time,' or pay attention to needs of other members of the family. Nowadays, it is common for Western mothers to put their babies into daycare, or the care of nannies or 'au pairs,' by a few months of age. In this way, we start to encourage that there be space between mother and child, starting early in infancy.

A Western parent does not hold onto or try to direct an individuating child when he starts to crawl or toddle away from her. She encourages the infant and toddler to crawl, walk, move outward, and explore on his own (after eliminating foreseeable dangers that a child of this age could not recognize). She says, "It's OK! Don't worry, I'm here watching, and I'll help if you need me. You can count on me, check back with me, and share with me. If I'm not where you can see me, I'll be in the next room or downstairs within earshot, where I'll hear you. Or I'll hear you on the intercom." A Western mother continues to be attentive and supportive, but her contact is at times acoustic and from a distance rather than being proximate, in direct visual or physical contact. Alternately, she may say, "Don't worry if I'm out, because I'm leaving you with a good caretaker who will look after you, and I'll be back soon." Her assumption is that the child will be safe moving off toward the unknown, learning to sit, walk, run, and explore things, because she will be watching, appreciating him from a distance, and supporting him in his adventure. "You can check back with me when you need to, or bring me things to show me." The child has his or her own room, bed, and belongings. Our ideal is to foster a child's growing autonomy and feeling competent by our encouraging and appreciative exclamations of, "Good job!"

Against this background of our encouragement individual autonomy, and freedom of thought and of speech, we expect our children to mature, develop discretion and appropriate judgment concerning truth and falsehood, and become able to regulate their behavior in ways that are (within broad guidelines) socially appropriate and empathic toward others.

In the two other cultures that we will be considering, parents seek to curtail a growing child's autonomy and to more narrowly channel the child's individuation. In each case, there is no flexibility for an individual to decide whether or not to lie or dissemble in circumstances where culturally dictated falsification is mandatory. In Japan, from the time that a child starts school and becomes part of an extrafamilial peer group, it is mandatory that she or he consciously pretend, put on a 'mask' that hides and belies all inner thoughts and personal feelings, and strictly adhere to a prescribed 'act' or deceptive role that everyone must play in *all* public relationships.[10] In Eskimo (or Inuit) culture, parents and other adults systematically enact dramatized deceptions that tease, mislead, and traumatize infants and toddlers, resulting in an arrest in the children's development that has survival value for individuals and the community within their unusual harsh Arctic environment.[11]

The 'Front Side' in Japan

A Japanese mother traditionally had an exclusive and continuous intimate relationship with her youngest baby that excluded her husband and her older children and continued through the early subphases of separation and individuation (Mahler et al., 1975). Within the mother-child dyad, cognitive individuation was encouraged while spatial separation was discouraged. The infant was encouraged to be curious, to look outward, and to master the surround (including becoming sensitive to the cultural mores and expectations of people beyond the dyad) while remaining on his mother's lap, held back and discouraged from spatially moving away.

A child would remain in direct physical contact with mother through the differentiation, practicing early rapprochement subphases of separation-individuation. During these stages (up to about age three), the mother and child did not often let go of one another's hand or clothing or lose sight of one another. If the child wanted to go somewhere, he would grab mother by the hand and try to pull her to go with him or ask her to pick him up and carry him while he pointed which way to go. If a child would want to move away autonomously and go off by himself, the mother would hold onto him and pull him back to stay with her.

Ultimately, however, the birth of a younger infant might disrupt this exclusive intimacy, and the now second-to-youngest child would be displaced from his position of unique privilege and suddenly dethroned. Alternately, if a younger infant did not come along, the special relationship with mother would become disrupted when the individuating child violated the "Don't look!" taboo concerning knowledge about genitality, causing the mother to very abruptly suddenly withdraw, ending the child's special relationship with her (Kitayama 1985, 1991).[12]

When children abruptly and involuntarily lost their unique intimate position with mother, it then became essential that they totally control any expression of their panicky internal turmoil and rage (that they feel has injured mother and caused her withdrawal), or they would be ostracized by everyone else as well because disruptive behavior and making noise by crying are intolerable to and not accepted by others. The previous permit for complete freedom to express oneself has now been cancelled. Two central myths of the traditional Japanese Shinto and Buddhist religions—the myths of Susano-o and Ajase—focus on this traumatic period of transition. Each mythical hero was ostracized by the outside world when he became stormy, raging, and intrusive after having been dethroned and losing his infantile omnipotence. In the modern era, when a child leaves the infantile world of omnipotence she or he starts to go to school, where conforming to one's group of peers and respect for the teacher and other elders becomes mandatory and essential. A favorite saying henceforth is, "A nail that sticks up gets hammered down." The child is left with deep inner feelings of both shame and guilt, blaming himself for having bodily injured and humiliated his hitherto self-sacrificing mother and having driven her away. He or she tries to find a way to contain their own tumultuous inner feelings of self-blame and to repair the damage, but they feel unable to do so. Fears of being shamed and ostracized by others if their hurtful thoughts and inner turmoil are discovered, loss of self-esteem, and attempts to restore narcissistic balance become major components of subsequent impulse regulation.[13]

Under the pressure of adults' expectations for self-control, and in collaboration with their peers, they force themselves to comply with and adhere to a 'false self' veneer, a false-face mask, or a scripted role of pretense to respectability and propriety that the group prescribes for them to enact in public. In effect, henceforth they comply with public expectations, falsifying and being untrue to their authentic inner self, creating a public persona that is like an actor playing a scripted role on an open stage.[14] They consciously experience two different aspects or portions of their self that they refer to as their "front side" (inauthentic public personality) and their "back side" (inner true self).

The needs of the inner true self do not get totally and permanently ignored, however. As long as one behaves in an adequately socialized way in public, one can periodically regress into refueling with a mother-substitute, in 'Amae,' a temporary culturally-sanctioned replication and reenactment of the original state of dependent intimacy and shared omnipotence of early childhood (Doi 1962, 1973; Taketomo, 1986, Freeman, 1998).

It is very difficult to function in Japan unless one is part of a group or community. One's front side public persona must conform to the mores of and support the honor of the group. It is not only acceptable but mandatory to contrive and to falsify when necessary in order to support and maintain the group's public image and esteem. Nonconformity or a serious step out of line is not only shameful, but risks ostracism, being severed from the group or community as a pariah, and becoming isolated from everyone.

Although people's public posture and relationships become contrived and inauthentic, the Japanese continue to be individuated, thoughtful, and autonomous in their inner world of thoughts and feelings. They can't confide in, or share these personal inner thoughts and real feelings with another member of their group or social milieu, or even a close Japanese colleague; but they have no problem talking about their inner feelings to an outsider who becomes a friend, and can also become comfortable to do so in therapy once they trust the neutrality and confidentiality of the psychotherapeutic process. A respected neutral psychotherapist who has no contact with the patient's own social milieu, becomes a confidant.

Eskimo (Inuit) Teasing Dramas

Whereas we in our culture tend to try to do everything we can to enhance a child's individuation and progress toward autonomously exploring and discovering things, each in his or her own way, this is not desirable in all cultures. Inuit (or Eskimo) parents, for example, do not want their children to discover things in their own unique way. For reasons of survival in their extremely harsh Arctic environment, they arrest children's development in the pre-oedipal period, in the latter portion of what we call the rapprochement crisis, just at the beginning of the road toward preliminary self and object constancy (Mahler et al., 1975). Inuit personality subsequently remains fixated or arrested at that point in pre-oedipal development. Although the Inuit do have intrapsychic and personality manifestations that derive from the biological genital phase, Inuit children never get into what we would recognize as an oedipal conflict and its resolution. As a result of their modified pattern of intrapsychic development, Eskimos continue, through adulthood, to be prone to severe dissociative attacks of acute separation panic (known as Pibloktoq or 'Arctic Hysteria') if they are separated from their mother, their home, or a mother-representative. In these attacks, they run amok, endangering their own lives, evoking pursuit and rescue by their colleagues (Foulks, Freeman, and Freeman 1978; Freeman, Foulks, and Freeman 1978).

The child-rearing practices of the Inuit contribute to this alteration in intrapsychic development. These include a systematic use of pretense, enacted dramatizations, and make-believe falsifications that traumatically tease, torment, and upset the child during the separation-individuation process, altering the child's development. The modifications in intrapsychic development are ones that Inuit culture, over many generations, has found to be not only useful but essential to survival in the unbelievably harsh Arctic environmental circumstances to which Eskimos successfully adapted and in which they have survived and thrived.

The Eskimo male infant has often been perceived to be a reincarnation of a previous relative who was a great hunter. The parents watch for and seek to discover traits of this ancestor reemerging in the young infant and are excited to discover behavior which will later be adaptive for the boy's future role as a hunter. But most other forms of autonomous assertive behavior are discouraged in infants and young children.

Starting shortly after birth, Inuit mothers traditionally begin a pattern of challenging their child with ambivalent so-called 'affectionate teasing' (Briggs, 1971) of their infants. This might include upsetting the infant by making the baby uncomfortable or frightening him to the point of tears.

Then, just as the baby's face begins to screw up and tears come to his eyes, the mother laughs affectionately and comforts the baby. Mothers say that a crying baby "wants to be the boss, and that is no good." The infant experiences maternal stiffness and disappointment if he expresses unacceptable affect, and conversely feels mother's approval and is given warmth if he or she calms down quickly without crying. The baby strives to control aggressive or assertive behavior, in order to elicit her affection.

By the second half of the first year, the baby begins to differentiate, starts to locomote, and seeks at times to separate from mother and to move away. The Inuit mother feels uncomfortable concerning the child's assertiveness and discourages autonomous exploratory behavior. Every effort is made to both limit autonomous activity by distracting the child towards more passive activities, and to keep the infant still and quiet, often on the mother's back inside her parka where his or her movements and behaviors are highly restrained (Briggs, 1971). The mother is intolerant of angry feelings in the child, and she attempts to gain control of the infant's hostility through the 'affectionate teasing' in which she evokes a negative affect in the child but then stops just prior to the point of its overt expression. The child may be provoked to intense frustration and anger, but the mother does not accept the child expressing these feelings.

By the time the child is a toddler, the mother's relationship with the child changes. She continues to set up teasing and frightening enactments to challenge the child, but now gets *others* to play the role of teasing or scaring the child while she serves as the child's 'rescuer.' The child is confronted with upsetting fictional dramatizations and unfounded shaming confrontations by visiting adults, kin, friends, and older siblings. The toddler's mother looks on while others utilize dissembling and pretense to provoke the child; and then, when the child is tormented to the point of becoming upset (with perhaps tears and screaming if the child is teased by older siblings), the mother becomes the toddler's rescuer and comforter. A child is led to perceive his social world as dangerous, and clings even more to the protective comfort provided by mother. After the child is about three years old, the mother tries to become less protective, preferring the child to not experience himself as too strong, but rather as continuing to be weak and vulnerable to sanctions and dangers. This contributes to the child's continuing to be dependent on her.

The staged enactments of frightening and shaming bad objects sensitize the child to the dangers of separation from mother and lead to the child clinging to an image of the 'good mother.' Increasing sensitivity to shame and ridicule make him anxious about social interactions and autonomous forms of activity which are not acceptable. This results in the child's inability to ultimately resolve the ambitendency of the rapprochement crisis and to move onward toward libidinal object constancy and self-constancy. Eskimos remain bound to the role of being 'the apple of their mother's eye,' dependent constantly on the presence of their mother or a mother substitute in order to maintain a feeling of safety and well-being.[15]

The child deals with ambivalent feelings by joining with the other members of his culture in their joint pretense of splitting off the pent-up frustrated and aggressive components and projecting them outside onto imaginary figures. This fiction makes it possible to purify an idealized image of mother and not be endangered by rage. In Alaska, the projected hostile images may take the form of "little men," the *tuniks* (white men), or other persecutory beings who are waiting to harm children who have strayed too far from their mothers. The mother reinforces this projection and uses the child's fear of the imaginary figures in her efforts to control the child. She tells him that he must do the right things or "The tuniks will come and get you!" "Tuniks *love* children who do *that!*"

The idealized image of the mother springs from the child's continuing dependence on her. Rather than asserting personal autonomy and pushing away on his own, he strives to maintain her affection and admiration by achieving mastery in maternally and culturally sanctioned roles, becoming the apple of her eye. An Eskimo boy seeks to live out his mother's dreams and fulfill her expectations for the adult she wishes him to become, a hunter who successfully provides crucial sustenance for his family.

Later, while hunting far from home, the Eskimo hunter projects an imaginary image of mother onto his entire surrounding environment. As long as he is working and striving to live up to his mother's ideal and fulfilling the role that she defined for him, he carries his idealized image of mother with him and experiences her as being immanent and omnipresent. This allows him to feel safe, enveloped in her arms, even when far away from home.

Why would a culture develop and sustain a pattern, over many generations, of raising children in this way? For countless generations, an Eskimo hunter often had to go out alone with his dog sled searching for food in the winter. He and his family would not survive if he did not get food—that is, not only *find* food, but also successfully bring it *back* to his home and his family. If he did not succeed or did not return, the family would die. Family-lines that have survived have all, for multiple generations, had this same experience. A hunter goes out into rolling dunes of wind-blown snow. In the Arctic winter it is dark twenty-four hours of the day, with perhaps (if it is not cloudy and snowing) a little bit of dim light from the aurora borealis. He travels many miles until he finds some game . . . but then he has to find his way back home. There are no roads or road maps, or street signs . . . nothing but trackless blowing and shifting snow dunes. There may be one or several blizzards. Yet if he doesn't find game and bring it back, the family will not survive (Carpenter, 1955, 1973).

The families that have an advantage to survive in this environment are those families whose hunters have retained the enhanced special capacities of a practicing subphase child whose entire life is organized around exploring, discovering, categorizing perceptions, and finding his way in an initially unknown amorphous spatial surround. Toddlers focus upon a puzzle similar to the one that faces the Inuit hunter—the problem of conceptualizing and getting a grasp of one's relative and changing position in space—and toddlers have a tremendous hypertrophy of the capacities that are necessary to solve these particular problems. Inuit hunters can also bask in the protection of a toddler's feeling of invulnerability as long as they hold onto regressive imaginative access to the world of dual unity with mother and shared magical omnipotence (Mahler et al., 1975).

The systematic use of lying, deception, and falsehood to stress an Inuit boy and to slow down his development has had an advantage in that it preserves and enhances the aptitudes and special characteristics of the practicing subphase. Traumatizing the child with falsified dramatizations and arresting development at a stage prior to a rapprochement resolution turns out to have been an effective way of child rearing for people whose survival depended upon optimizing and preserving these particular capacities into adulthood. These qualities became central pillars of existence, crucial for the way of life that Eskimos have lived.

Similarly in the case of an Inuit girl's development, discouraging the development of excessively individuated autonomy and maintaining her dependence on her mother's and family's approval, while preserving as much of the optimistic resiliency of her practicing subphase as possible, supported a girl as she undertook the extremely difficult roles she had to fulfill as a woman in persevering and sustaining her family through the harsh circumstances of their environment.

Perhaps surprisingly, we find that conscious falsification and the staging of false dramatizations, deceptively presented to the naïve infant and young child as being 'true,' and traumatic enough to cause an arrest in development may make a culturally valued contribution to intrapsychic development in certain circumstances.

Concluding Remarks

For some cultures, what is inauthentic may be better in certain circumstances than what is real. Cultures sometimes sanction a major situational or systematic use of dishonesty and inauthenticity, when it is felt that this will serve adaptive or altruistic goals.

In our culture, lying about the Stork and about the Serpent in the Garden of Eden or telling White Lies are better than telling the truth. Japanese culture traditionally required older children and young adults to suppress their true inner selves and become deceptive role players, dissemblers, and pretenders in their public relationships. The child's earlier 'permit' for freedom of expression and gratification is suddenly revoked, and the old 'truths' are suddenly no longer true! Henceforth, in public, one must live a lie. Suddenly there is a shift of the locus of decision-making from oneself, as the adored active young child within a dyad of special privilege, to outside forces to whom one is forced to submit and whom one tries to appease by inauthentic pretending and dissembling, following alien rules. The only 'truth' now is that one must hide one's inner turmoil, comply, and try to somehow make amends rather than being 'true' to one's mortifying inner tumultuous self.

On the other hand, socially-syntonic pretending and lying in one's public posture in dealing with others is ego-syntonic insofar as it helps an individual to self-regulate and to not reveal inner feelings of blameworthiness and shame. It offers an external role model and social structure that one can rely upon until one can gradually start to neutralize dependent longings and aggressive impulses through recurrent opportunities for rapprochement refueling in 'amae,' start to resolve the inner feelings of shame and culpability, regain narcissistic balance, and mature into becoming a nurturing grandparent and elder who looks after and gives 'amae' to others (Freeman, 1998).

Cultural uses of untruths and lying that at first glance may seem to be pathogenic turn out to be beneficial and to have unexpected authenticity and value when understanding them by examining their contexts more closely.

Notes

1. The Adventures of Pinocchio, by Carlo Collodi published in 1883.

2. On the front page of the Weekend Edition of the *Wall Street Journal*, on August 2–3, 2008, Pinocchio's nose is featured stretched across the top of the page, above the paper's logo, with a subtitle: "Do you lie to pollsters?" In Tokyo, we bought pocket measuring tapes shaped to look like Pinocchio's face in profile. In order to bring out the tape, one pulls Pinocchio's nose and stretches it longer.

3. Unpublished papers by William Singletary and Ann Smolen presented at the American Psychoanalytic Association Discussion Group on Myths and Children's Stories: "Pinocchio, Growth and Transformation in Psychoanalysis," on January 18, 2006.

4. Cultures differ, for example, even in their fundamental conception of the passage of time. Does time progress in a unidirectional linear flow, from the past through the present toward the future, as Westerners have believed? Or is it nonlinear? Is it part of a 'space-time continuum,' as Einstein suggested, and does it bend like light waves have been found to bend? Or, as many Asian cultures believe, does time in fact recycle like the recurring seasons, or blossoms that bloom and fade but return again next spring? Is time like the sun that sets in the evening, depriving the world of its heat and light, but rises again at the dawn of the next day? Do we live only once, or are we reborn? If so, are we reborn just once, into an ultimate Heaven or Hell, or are we resurrected or reincarnated through a series of rebirths and life cycles?

5. Patricia A. Freeman contributed to the cross-cultural research upon which this paper was based.

6. At the annual Margaret Mahler Symposium in Philadelphia on 4–26–08, Bert Ruttenberg offered an example of how cultural change has affected us: "Look how much our culture has *changed* since 1954, when attorney Joseph Welch electrified the country during the televised Army-McCarthy Hearings, by dramatically confronting Senator Joeseph McCarthy, saying, 'Senator!! *Have* you no *shame??!*' . . . However, *today*, it seems like nobody pays any *attention* to shame!"

7. Spitz (1972) has graphically described this as the infant casting bridges outward, into the darkness, toward a distant shore.

8. I have reviewed some culturally sanctioned instances of falsification and lying to children being practiced in our culture. There are other instances where parental lying that involves a child may not be altruistic, considerate, or culturally acceptable, but rather self-serving on the part of the parent and potentially harmful for the child. For example, in dysfunctional divorcing families, the children may be treated as puppets if a parent tries to manipulate them into lying to the court in order to defame the child's other parent.

9. A Japanese colleague, Masahisa Nishizono, past president of the Japanese Psychoanalytic Society, describes Western culture as 'a culture of nomadism.' Autonomous thinking has been a Western ideal since Abraham and Moses contributed to the foundations of Western culture when they each left the respective lands of their parents in order to discover and to found something new and better.

10. Kitayama, 1985, 1988, 1991, 1996; Freeman, 1996.

11. Briggs, 1971; Foulks, 1972; Foulks, Freeman, and Freeman, 1978; Freeman, Foulks, and Freeman, 1978.

12. The abrupt change was similar to exile from the Garden of Eden, after a child had been accustomed to paradise for his or her entire lifetime. But since the Japanese child's possession of mother had been more exclusive, continuous, and intense, the fall from grace is much steeper.

13. Kitayama, 1991, 1996.

14. Kitayama, personal communication.

15. As was mentioned earlier, they continue, through adulthood, to be prone to severe Pibloktoq attacks of acute separation panic if they are separated from their mother, their home, or a mother-representative. In these attacks, they run amok, endangering their own lives, and evoking pursuit and rescue by their colleagues.

References

Briggs, J.L. (1971). *Never in Anger*. Cambridge, MA: Harvard University Press.

Carpenter, E.S. (1955). Eskimo space concepts. In: *Explorations 5: Studies in Culture and Communication*, ed. E.S. Carpenter, pp. 131–145. Toronto: University of Toronto Press.

Carpenter, E.S. (1973). *Eskimo Realities*. New York: Holt, Rinehart and Winston.

Collodi, C. (1892). *The Adventures of Pinocchio: Story of a Puppet*. Reprint Edition (1991). Berkeley and Los Angeles, University of California Press.

Doi, T. (1962). Amae: A Key Concept for Understanding Japanese Personality Structure." In: R. J. Smith and R.K. Beardsley, eds., *Japanese Culture: Its Development and Characteristics*. Chicago: Aldine.

Doi, T. (1973). *The Anatomy of Dependence*. Tokyo: Kodansha.

Erickson, E.H. (1959). *Identity and the Life Cycle*, New York: International Universities Press

Foulks, E.F., Freeman, D.M.A., and Freeman, P.A. (1978). Pre-oedipal dynamics in a case of Eskimo arctic hysteria, In: *The Psychoanalytic Study of Society*, Volume 8, W. Muensterberger, B., Boyer, and A. Esman, eds., pp. 41–69. New Haven, CT: Yale University Press.

Freeman, D.M.A. (1996). Nyuyoji no hattatu to haji no taiken (Child dDevelopment and shame experiences"). In: *Haji (Shame)*, O. Kitayama, ed., pp. 65–102. Tokyo: Seiwa Shoten.

Freeman, D.M.A. (1998). Emotional refueling in development, mythology, and cosmology: the Japanese separation-individuation experience. In: S. Akhtar and S. Kramer, eds, *The Colors of Childhood*, pp. 17–60. New York: Jason Aronson.

Freeman, D.M.A., Foulks, E.F., and Freeman, P.A. (1978). Child development and arctic hysteria in the north Alaskan Eskimo male. *The Journal of Psychological Anthropology* I: 2, 203–210.

Freud, A. (1965). *Normality and Pathology in Childhood*. New York: International Universities Press.

Kitayama, O. (1985). Preoedipal 'taboo' in Japanese folk tragedies. *International Review of Psycho-Analysis* 12: 173–185.

Kitayama, O. (1988). Forced guilt. *Japanese Journal of Psycho-Analysis* 32: 117–123.

Kitayama, O. (1991). The wounded caretaker and guilt. *International Review of Psycho-Analysis* 18: 229–240.

Kitayama, O. (1996). *Haji (Shame)*. Tokyo: Seiwa Shoten.

Kitayama, O. (1998). Transience: its beauty and danger. *International Journal of Psychanalysis*, Vol., 79 Part 5, 937–953.

Mahler, M.S., Pine, F., and Bergman, A. (1975). *The Psychological Birth of the Human Infant: Symbiosis and Individuation*. New York: Basic Books.

Roiphe, H. and Galenson, E. (1981). *Infantile Origins of Sexual Identity*. New York: International Universities Press.

Spitz, R.A. (1972). Bridges: on anticipation, duration and meaning," *Journal of the American Psychoanalytic Association* 20: 721–735.

Taketomo, Y. (1986). Amae as metalanguage: a critique of Doi's theory of amae. *Journal of the American Academy of Psychoanalysis* 14: 525–544.

Winnicott, D.W. (1971). *Playing and Reality*. London, Tavistock.

~

CHAPTER NINE

Cultures of Dishonesty: From Hidden Cancers and Concealed Selves to Politics and Poker

Mark Moore, Ph.D.

In the beginning of his chapter on socio-cultural perspectives on dishonesty and lying, Dr. Freeman relates the tale of Pinocchio. The tale exemplifies aspects of the Western ideal of supportive parenting that allows children to discover for themselves what is true and false in the world. In similar fashion I will begin with an Eastern European tale I heard told at a workshop on adjusting to life in a foreign culture.

The Tale of the Dreaming Woodsman

A woodsman, living in isolation in the forest, dreams of a treasure chest buried outside the walls of the capital city. He has this dream night after night with increasing vividness, and it haunts his every waking moment. Eventually he can bear it no longer and he feels compelled to take the long trip to the city and test the veracity of what he dreams.

Once the woodsman arrives there he is startled to find a spot outside the city walls that is almost exactly as he dreamt it; the only difference is that there is a soldier posted close by, guarding one of the smaller entrances to the city. The woodsman is afraid to start digging with the soldier present, but now he is also convinced of the truth of his dream. He waits hour after hour, hoping for the guard to leave, and all the while a tense, growing despair mounts in him that he will never be able to unearth his treasure unobserved.

All this time, the guard has been watching this man and he noted the man's tense pacing, the frequent stealthy glances in his direction, and his growing agitation. Both suspicious and curious he approaches the man and demands to know his business. The man, unaccustomed to stern uniformed authority and almost at his wit's end, breaks down in sobs and begs forgiveness for what is a fool's errand.

The soldier sympathetically assures the man that he has done no wrong and asks what ails him. The woodsman tells him of his dream, his compulsion to heed its message and his despair to have come so far for naught. The soldier laughs and tells the man that only fools follow their dreams. "Why, I myself have been on night watch these past few days and my restless dreams are ever the same and quite compelling. Every time I sleep, I dream of a small hut in the forest with an oak door and deer antlers across the entrance. There is a giant hearthstone by the back wall, and each night I dream of digging under that hearthstone and finding a great treasure. But what a fool I would be to place faith in such a dream—my life and future are here as a guard, not chasing some fantasy." "Aye," agrees the woodsman with a gleam in his eye, "and you helped me see where my own future best lies." With that he took leave of the soldier and began to make his way home, to his hut in the forest with its oaken door, the antlers over its entrance and the ancient hearthstone by the back wall, under which lay the treasure he had dreamt of.

Starting Out From Home

The purpose of that tale when first told to me was to emphasize how one often needs to travel far from home to truly appreciate what is close at hand. In my response to Dr. Freeman's paper I hope to highlight how his description of dishonesty and lying in Japanese and Inuit cultures enriches our own understanding of such issues in Western culture. Indeed, Dr. Freeman in his introduction notes that by clarifying how cultural vantage points shape the boundaries between truthfulness and lying, we are better able to consider how that process occurs in our own culture.

Hiding and Revealing in Child Development

Dr. Freeman's starting point is a discussion of make-believe and the balance of hiding and revealing that is part of child development in Western culture. He describes how infants in their first year begin to differentiate between what is trustable and what is untrustworthy as they look beyond the symbiotic milieu of mother and child. From their second year on, the influence of culture through language is evident in children's categories of what is true and false. Contrasting opposites and contradictions are addressed through pretense and make-believe.

Dr. Freeman points out that cultures differ in their perception of what is true versus false; those occasions when it is socially expected that one lie; of pretense and role-playing as acceptable rather than fraudulent or inauthentic; and when it is constructive for parents to lie to children. White lies are given as an example of culturally condoned lying and the important point is made that people typically seek a middle ground between cultural mores and personal discretion.

White Lies and Cancer

Each culture strives for a balance between hiding and revealing. As an example, Dr. Freeman notes how discussions of anatomical differences and sexuality involve culturally condoned misrepresentations meant to protect children. Misrepresentations are also commonly employed with children when parents have a serious illness, such as cancer, and the argument is often made in such cases that misrepresentation is in the best interest of the child. However, as with anatomical differences and sexuality, we should not blind ourselves to the possibility of self-protective motivations of the behalf of the adults.

Quite often in my work with cancer patients, I am confronted with patients' concern that their children should not be exposed to the worry and fear inherent in knowing that a parent has cancer. However, children are adept at picking up on unspoken cues and the side effects and general disruption created by chemotherapy and/or radiation are near impossible to fully conceal, not to mention the gargantuan effort required of the parents if they are to adequately mask their own distress. In one study of children's worries about their mother's breast cancer, Zahlis (2001) stressed how school-age "children not only tried to make sense of what they heard but also of what they saw" (p. 1024). Armsden and Lewis (1993) argued that a child's sense of security in relation to a parents' illness is threatened when the illness makes the parent unavailable, and that children have difficulty differentiating their parent's emotional response from their own. Physical and emotional availability cannot be fudged, however much we as parents may want to lie to ourselves or however much a child may be compelled to play along with our pretense. And the deep emotions felt in response to a cancer diagnosis are, in my experience, impossible to fully conceal.

I will often educate parents on these matters and explain that their children are likely responding to unspoken cues and further discussion will often reveal the parents' awareness of various emotional and behavioral cues that indicate the child's distress. I will explain age-appropriate ways to consider discussing illness with children and also how it is common for children to remain confused about cancer despite appropriate explanation. I will stress that they will require repeated assurances and clarifications.

At this point I am frequently confronted with resistance from the parents that requires a sensitive exploration of their own guilt for how they have burdened their family with their cancer and their profound anguish at the thought of upsetting their children. We often come to the realization that the parents themselves cannot bear confronting the reality of their own cancer as reflected in their children's concerns. It is a sad reminder of the complexity of motivation behind the white lies we often feel we have to tell our children.

Elusive Treasures in Faraway Lands

Dr. Freeman describes how Western mothers encourage individualizing children to move outward and explore their world and he emphasizes how they provide support through distant, acoustic contact. Space between mother and child is typically encouraged from early infancy as reflected in having a separate crib for children and our increasing comfort in using daycare or having babysitters watch our children. In contrast, parents in Japanese and Inuit cultures restrict a child's autonomy and place tight limits on their individuation. I will limit my comments to Dr. Freeman's section on Japanese culture, as my limited knowledge of the Inuit people would add little to what Dr. Freeman has already written.

Japanese Culture and the Development of *Omote*
A key difference in Japanese child-rearing practices, as noted by Dr. Freeman, is that children are kept in direct physical contact with the mother throughout the differentiation, practicing, and early rapprochement subphases of separation-individuation. Cognitive individuation is encouraged but not spatial separation—the child is encouraged to look outward and master the world while remaining on his mother's lap.

The exclusive intimacy between mother and child comes to an abrupt end and the child is expected to control his or her rage over their traumatic ejection from the state of privileged intimacy. The value placed on suppressing one's anger is reflected in the popular Japanese myths of Susano-o and Ajase, in which each hero is ostracized after becoming enraged once dethroned and stripped of infantile omnipotence.

Dr. Freeman describes how conformity to one's peers and respect for elders becomes a valued trait as a Japanese child enters school. Emphasized in

Dr. Freeman's description is the notion that impulse regulation then derives from fear of shame and ostracism, loss of self-esteem and a striving for narcissistic balance. Later pressure in adult life to maintain self-control contributes to the development of *omote* ("front side") or a public persona that, according to Dr. Freeman, is untrue to their authentic inner self. Individuals are required to lie for the sake of the group's public image and esteem, and the needs of the true self are only met periodically through the regressive experience of *amae*, which is an acceptable reenactment of childhood dependency.

I agree in part with Dr. Freeman's view of the cost to the individual and by extension the wider society when the expression of private truths is actively discouraged, or when the nail that sticks out gets hammered down. A grim example of such is evident in Japan's recent history. In December 1937 the Japanese army entered Nanking and over the course of six brutal weeks proceeded to torture, mutilate, rape, and massacre the population, resulting in the deaths of over 300,000 Chinese civilians (Chang, 1997).

The continued denial of the extent of these atrocities, and of the responsibility of the Japanese forces for what occurred, is a chilling example of the value placed on maintaining group esteem in Japan. Chang (1997) provides recent examples of leading politicians such as Ishihara Shintaro, who stated that the massacre was a story made up by the Chinese, and Kajiyama Seiroku, the Japanese chief cabinet secretary who claimed that the sex slaves and rape victims of the Japanese army were willing prostitutes. Yet it would be naïve and insulting to presume that conformist denial and dishonesty are the measure of Japanese society. Take the example of Ienaga Saburo who, in 1965, sued the Japanese government when the ministry of education tired to interfere with his attempts to document the Nanking massacre in history texts for school children (Chang, 1997). Or Ono Kenji who has interviewed over two hundred rural farmers on their experiences as soldiers in Nanking (Chang, 1997). How are we to explain this, if we assume only negative pressures such as shame, guilt, and conformity to be factors in the development of a sense of an individuated self in Japan?

Ura and *Wa*: Japanese Concepts of the Private Self and Harmony

Dr. Freeman briefly notes that, in contrast to their *omote* or public posture, the Japanese are "individuated, thoughtful, and autonomous in their inner world of feelings." However, he does not elaborate on what developmental factors act as a counterweight to shame and fear of ostracism, and the dynamics inherent in the conflicting experiences of a private inner self and a public outer self. In a discussion of cultural differences in the experience of lying and dishonesty, one must consider the inner private experience that is at variance with the outer professed lie.

Two concepts are of help in considering this issue. The first of these is the concept of *ura*, or private experience (Doi, 1986). Literally, *ura* means back-side or flipside in contrast to *omote* which means "front-side." Takeo Doi (1986) in his book "The Anatomy of Self" notes that in classical Japanese *omote* means face and *ura* means mind or soul. Through an exploration of the various linguistic usages of these words he traces the dynamic interplay between front and back or face and mind, noting how the face expresses the mind or how the face hides the mind as expressed in the phrase: "Devil-mask, Buddha-mind."

It is tempting to dichotomize these two concepts. Winnicott's (1960) concepts of true and false self are especially tempting categories to use, but I agree with Doi that the one cannot exist without the other. Facial expression is no more inherently false than attempts at verbal expression of the mind are inherently true—most analysts would agree that the slightest grimace or quiver can say more than any word spoken in earnest, and words themselves are not to be taken at "face" value. *Omote* can reveal *ura* even in the very act of attempting to conceal it.

Notions of truth and authenticity, and of dishonesty and lying considered in the Japanese context become more complicated when we allow for the idea that presenting a seemingly compliant front-side to others does not necessitate disavowal of one's inner experience. The complex interplay between truth and lying is highlighted by a 14th century tale Doi (1986, pp. 42–43) quotes from Kenko's "Tsurezuregusa," in which a monk is explaining to a visitor why the people of Kyoto make promises that they do not intend to keep: "it is because they are gentle and they have human sympathy that they find it difficult to say no to what another has said . . . they do not mean to deceive, but since they are poor . . . there are doubtless many things in which they cannot carry out their true intentions." In contrast the hearts of the "people of the East are unkind" and because they are "blunt and unaffable, they do not hesitate to say no from the very beginning."

Doi comments that this failure to keep promises is not hypocritical but rather it serves to reduce tension between individuals, and this motivation to not disappoint the other may underlie Japanese fondness of "subtle considerations and delicate nuances in human relations" (Doi, 1986, p. 43). The idea that the motivation for presenting a "dishonest" front-side is out of consideration for the other, and not simply out of fear of shame and ostracism, is related to the second Japanese concept that I wish to introduce, namely the concept of *wa* or harmony.

The Japanese term *wa* is typically translated as harmony but its Japanese *kanji* (written form) is composed of two characters: the first character is the symbol for a rice stalk and the second character is the symbol for a mouth, implying a meaning of "fat and happy, peaceful, placid, tranquil or harmonious" (Walsh, 1969, p.75). One historical factor that elevated the importance of maintaining harmony in Japanese culture was the emphasis on the "family system" during the Tokugawa period (1600–1868) in which the system's purpose was "the ongoing welfare of the group as a whole, not the temporary aggrandizement of any member of it" (Mason and Caiger, 1997, p. 250). Consensus and the group's ultimate well-being were highly valued and disharmony spelt the end to the careful balance between benevolent authority and loyal service that ensured the family's survival. To that end, ambiguity in the expression of ideas was valued.

Alan Roland (1988) described the Japanese "familial self" as a psychological organization that facilitated the functioning of individuals within the "hierarchical intimacy relationships of the extended family, community and other groups" (p. 7). Such a family system is characterized by intense emotional connectedness and interdependence with permeable ego boundaries that allow for high levels of empathy and receptivity to others and a relational "we-self" sense of self. Nowhere is this more evident than in the child's early experience of intimacy with the mother. The desire for harmony in relations with others in adult life has its origins in the child enjoying the sense of shared identity with the mother.

Michael Balint, in his discussion of object and subject, referred to a "fantasy of primal harmony . . . which was destroyed either through our own fault, through the machinations of others, or by cruel fate" (1959, p. 64). It has its origins in a period of development in which "there are as yet no objects, although there is already an individual, who is surrounded, almost floats, in substances without exact boundaries; the substances and the individual mutually penetrate each other; that is, they live in a harmonious mix-up" (1959, p. 67).

Japanese conformity arises not only out of the shame and fear of ostracism that has its roots in the child's expulsion from the position of privileged intimacy with the mother, as Dr. Freeman implies. It also has earlier roots in the experience of looking out on the world from the vantage of the mother's lap, sharing a harmonious perspective in which the child feels safe and strong, sensing that the mother faces the same world too. The child's face (*omote*) is to the world but his mind (*ura*) is to his mother, deriving confidence from the face she shows to the world.

In later life, truth is not simply determined in the transitional space where one's face meets the world, but in the space where one's inner self—the backside or *ura*—turns to the face of the other, the face of the group. It is a space where nuance, sensitivity to the other and consideration determine what truth is most valued: not simply a public truth but the truth understood to exist between the self and those to whom we feel most connected.

A harmony arising out of shared *omote* or consensus implies an absence of impingement and it cannot always be simply equated with experiences of shame-driven or fear-based conformity. In harmonious experience with another, the self is felt to be embraced and ego boundaries are strengthened rather than weakened, and early positive experiences of commingled identity with the mother are reevoked. Instead of a potential cause of a loss of one's sense of self, harmony may be the means by which one's "private self" is more truly revealed and responded to in Japanese daily experience.

Treasures Under the Hearth

In discussing lies and dishonesty we are often at our most comfortable when we can cast it as a moral issue. Yet as Dr. Freeman's consideration of deception in Japanese and Inuit cultures has highlighted, the "simple" truth is not always the best course. Dr. Freeman's consideration of Inuit culture speaks for itself as a tantalizing and intriguing depiction of the role of deception in inhibiting autonomous exploration during the later period of the rapprochement crisis that may later serve to ensure an adult's survival in the Arctic. His paper challenges us to consider how lying and dishonesty serve an adaptive function—both for society as a whole and for the individual.

Dr. Freeman's paper forces us to reexamine our evaluation of the meaning and purpose of lies. In Japanese culture, not speaking one's mind can function to preserve group cohesion and prevent ostracism. I have argued that it can also provide subtle channels for the expression of *ura* or one's inner thoughts and feelings, and that it is also a means of evoking earlier ego-strengthening experiences of commingled identity with the mother. The Inuit culture utilizes a traumatic form of deceitful teasing that inhibits a child's autonomous exploration and binds the child closer to its mother. Dr. Freeman makes the case that such deceit contributes to a child's ability later in life to hunt successfully in the harsh Artic environment and, more importantly, to return home.

There are a few psychoanalytic authors who are willing to consider about the adaptive function of a lie although our natural inclination to be wary of liars on the couch is reflected in the title that O'Shaughnessy chose for her 1990 paper, "Can a liar be psycho-analysed?" O'Shaughnessy (1990) discusses a form of sadistic deception which has at its heart the wish to triumph over the analyst and which serves the function of managing castration anxiety.

Lemma (2005) considers two further forms of self-preservative lying. In the first form, the liar experiences the object as emotionally unavailable or inscrutable and experiences anxiety with regard to loss of the object's love. The lies that are told in this case allow for the creation of a lovable version of the self to present to the object or can elicit the object's concern through invented danger. In the second form the liar experiences the object as intrusive and feels threatened with a form of claustrophobic anxiety. Lies told in this case are used to divert the object or to erect a boundary between the self and the object. In both forms the author highlights the adaptive dynamics of lying.

Back to the Society-At-Large

Outside of psychoanalysis, the wider culture also exhibits a disdain for liars and a professed discomfort with lying. The backlash against the Bush administration over their handling of intelligence regarding WMDs in Iraq or the scorn for Hillary Clinton's claim that she came under sniper gunfire during a trip to Bosnia as first lady in March 1996 indicate the public's aversion to dishonesty. However, our culture's ambivalence about lying and dishonesty is evidenced by our grudging acceptance that politics involves some form of dissemblance. As New York's governor, Mario Cuomo put it: "you campaign in poetry; you govern in prose;" and the electorate is often surprisingly forgiving of political "poetry." Bush was reelected despite the WMD debacle and Hillary Clinton's loss to Barack Obama did not pivot on exaggerated war stories.

In popular culture we see admiration of Hollywood antiheroes such as Paul Newman's and Robert Redford's con-artist characters in *The Sting*, Leonardo DiCaprio's check-forging character in *Catch Me If You Can*, and George Clooney's master of deceit in *Ocean's Eleven*. Even our greatest heroes often lead a duplicitous life, including such iconic American heroes as Superman, Spiderman, and Batman, spies such as Jason Bourne in the *Bourne* trilogy, and *Casablanca*'s Rick. And great evil must often be countered by clever deceit as exemplified by the central hero of *Schindler's List*.

Yet nowhere is popular admiration for the art of deception more evident than in the recent upsurge of national interest in poker. In 2003, amateur poker player Chris Moneymaker won the World Series of Poker against seasoned professional Sammy Farha. What made Moneymaker's win so awe-inspiring was not his tight playing style or his ability to read other players (indeed it could be argued that he was too impulsive a player); rather it was his willingness to pull off stone-cold bluffs against the best of them.

At the final table against Farha after eleven hours of playing and the clock coming up on 1.30 a.m., Moneymaker was dealt a king of spades and a seven of hearts; while Farha looked down to see a queen of spades and a nine of hearts. Moneymaker made a starting bet of 100,000 which Farha called. The next three shared cards were turned over to reveal a nine of spades, a two of diamonds, and a six of spades giving Farha the top pair with a pair of nines. Farha decided to play it cagily by checking (not betting), hoping that Moneymaker would think he had a weak hand. Moneymaker wisely chose to also check.

The fourth common card was turned over to reveal a third spade, the eight of spades, leaving both players one card short of a flush (five spades). It would be tempting for both of them to see that last card but Farha decided to make Moneymaker pay and he bet out 300,000, feeling rightfully confident with his pair of nines.

Farha had now put Moneymaker on the defensive as Moneymaker had to call that 300,000 if he was to stay in and try to catch a winning spade. Yet as the poker player Crandall Addington (as quoted by Alvarez, 1983) once put it, betting in no-limit poker is like shooting at a moving target only the target can start shooting back. And that is precisely what Moneymaker did, as he shot back with a semi-bluff bet of 500,000 on top of Farha's 300,000.

Moneymaker's inspired bluff made it appear that he was holding two spades in his hands that would make a flush with the three spades showing on the table. However, Farha was unconvinced and without hesitation he called the additional 500,000. The final card was turned over to reveal . . . nothing! A useless three of hearts was revealed that improved no one's hand but left Farha with the top pair of two nines. Moneymaker was looking at a hand of failed possibilities and at this point a lesser player would have walked away from the hand, folding to any bet Farha might make. Yet without a moment of hesitation, Moneymaker pushed all his remaining chips into the pot; a staggering 3.72 million dollars forcing Farha to a difficult decision. He had to determine if the flush that Moneymaker had represented on the last round of betting was indeed a reality that would cost Farha his entire chip pile of 2.97 million and the tournament title.

Moneymaker sat there, stone-faced; his entire World Series Championship resting on a bold-faced lie. Farha tried to needle a clue out of his opponent by asking: "You must have missed your flush, eh?" Moneymaker's utter lack of response caused Farha to go against his better judgment and he folded the winning hand. One can apply Lemma's (2005) concept of self-protective lying to describe how Moneymaker adaptively used deception to protect himself against the intrusive attacks of Farha and in the final moment to fend off Farha's correctly "omniscient" guess that Moneymaker had missed his flush and was merely bluffing. Moneymaker's deception was so successful that it was Farha who was left rattled and close to a million dollars poorer. A few hands later Farha lost the Championship by betting his entire pot on a pair of jacks against Moneymaker's two pairs.

Sometimes it must be conceded that there is sheer genius at play in the art of deception and games such as this exemplify why lying and dishonesty will always remain a respected and necessary part of our ego's armamentarium, and an acceptable and admired part of popular culture. In our individualized society, we may be scornful of what appears to be excessive self-deception and damaging group conformity in Japan or we may be disapproving of how Inuit mothers tease and deceive their children so as to reduce their autonomy. However, we too in Western culture readily utilize deception and lying in an adaptive fashion; for the protection of the individual against intrusive or unavailable others, as a means of self-regulation, for self-esteem, and as a means of triumphing over adversity.

Concluding Remarks

Dr. Freeman considered how differing cultural perspectives shape the distinction between truthfulness and lying, and in so doing he compelled us to consider the nature of lying and dishonesty in our own culture. He noted how all cultures strive for a balance between hiding and revealing the truth to children and white lies were given as an example of culturally condoned lying. I elaborated upon the role of white lies in the decisions parents make when they have cancer, and how their conscious wish to protect their child from knowing too much can also disguise their own profound discomfort in acknowledging their own fears about their disease.

Dr. Freeman's description of the developmental roots of group conformity in Japan and the cost to one's sense of inner authenticity emphasizes the fear of ostracism and shame that derives from the child's abrupt expulsion from a position of privileged intimacy with the mother. I expanded upon this idea and explained how the Japanese concepts of private self and harmony provide an alternative model for understanding the importance and value of group consensus, even if the cost is a conflict between private truth and public truth.

Teasing and deliberate deception are used in Inuit child-rearing practices and Dr. Freeman discusses their impact on an adult's capacity to survive in the Arctic environment. In turn I consider briefly the popular acceptance of deception and lying within our own culture and how they are not always vilified attributes. Indeed they are abilities that are often admired, adaptive, and necessary.

References

Alvarez, A. (1983). *The Biggest Game in Town*. San Francisco: Chronicle Books.

Armsden, G.C. and Lewis, F.M. (1993). The child's adaptation to parental medical illness: theory and clinical implications. *Patient Education and Counseling* 22: 153–165.

Balint, M. (1959). *Thrills and Regressions*. London: The Hogarth Press.

Chang, I. (1997). *The Rape of Nanking*. New York: Basic Books.

Doi, T. (1986). *The Anatomy of the Self*. Tokyo: Kodansha International Ltd.

Lemma, A. (2005). The many faces of lying. *International Journal of Psychoanalysis* 86: 737–753.

Mason, R.H.P. and Caiger, J.G. (1997). *A History of Japan: Revised Edition*. Rutland, VT: Charles E. Tuttle Company, Inc.

O'Shaughnessy, E. (1990). Can a liar be psychoanalysed? *International Journal of Psychoanalysis* 71: 187–195.

Roland, A. (1988). *In Search of the Self in India and Japan*. Princeton, NJ: Princeton University Press.

Walsh, L. (1969). *Read Japanese Today*. Rutland, VT: Charles E. Tuttle Company, Inc.

Winnicott, D.W. (1960). Ego distortion in terms of true and false self. In:*The Maturational Processes and the Facilitating Environment*. pp.140–152. New York: International Universities Press, 1965

Zahlis, E.H. (2001). The child's worries about the mother's breast cancer: sources of distress in school-age children. *Oncology Nursing Forum* 28: 1019–1025.

~

CHAPTER TEN

Distortions of Truth from White Lies to Mass Murder: A Concluding Commentary

Henri Parens, M.D.

Considerations of "Dishonesty, Lying, and Inauthenticity" cover a wide range of distortions of truth. Here I will predominantly use the single factor, *truth*; but in the sense in which I am using it, I could equally use the factor, *reality*, and occasionally I will. Each noun, *dishonesty, lying, inauthenticity*, has its distinct features even as each distorts the *truth*. But even considering all these sins under the umbrella of "distortions of the truth" we face an essential uncertainty. Can we start with the assumption that "the truth" is always true? Psychoanalysts know that what we experienced and remember is not simply determined by historical truth; from it, we each forge our distinctive "narrative truth" (Spence, 1982). Corollary to "truth," even "reality" is well established to be subjective. It is not just the philosophers (e.g., Immanuel Kant) who hold this to be true; psychoanalysts too know that the reality that governs our individual life is not 'absolute reality' but how we *experience* that absolute reality, *subjectively*; that it truly is our 'psychic reality.' And we know that it is our psychic reality that governs our thoughts and behaviors. Only in math, is *truth* true: 2 + 2 cannot equal anything but 4. 4 is the *truth*.

Thinkers in all disciplines know that truth and reality are for the most part subjective. In film this has been portrayed in the Japanese classic, Akira Kurosawa's *Rashomon*, wherein three persons witness an accident and report it in accord with their experience of it. Convincingly rendered, the three witnesses report significantly differing *truths*.

Daniel Freeman (this volume) holds, cogently, that different cultures hold different truths to be 'self-evident.' He tells us that "different cultures' perceptions of truth . . . vary widely," that these are determined by "beliefs," and that these differ among differing cultures. Freeman suggests that "cultural [determinations] shape the cognitive and affective dimensions of what is considered to be either [observable fact, inherent immutable truth—like our own Declaration of Independence truths which we believe to be 'self-evident'—acceptable make-belief, socially-expected constructive falsification, or] purposefully misleading . . . falsehood condemnable as lying" (this volume).

But cultures change, Freeman tells us, and are doing so in an accelerated pace given the "communication and transportation revolutions" that have led to so much "intermingling of people." We now know the world over, that no *Homo sapiens* have tails, that we are much more alike than was once assumed. But in addition, Freeman points out, within cultures children grow up in a world very different than that of their own parents and certainly their grandparents. This is evident in all spheres of life. In the domain of world-wide immigrations, it brings its problems at a societal level to be sure, but also at a familial level; we see it especially in the difficulties that are unavoidably present in the intergenerational challenges that emerge within immigrant families, a finding amply documented (e.g., Akhtar, 1999). But this change in cultures, I would say evolution of cultures, also has some large positive potential for change in our world that may benefit human existence, that may even eliminate some of the evils that come from some coerced cultural 'beliefs'—which I will briefly address below. And documenting Freeman's point about changes that come from generational evolution, it has its delightful moments. As a child analyst, I have learned to accept the fact that my child patients are going to tell me about games, television programs, and books I have never even heard of. They are surprised, some are disappointed; I chuckle and find it an opportunity to tell the child that he can teach me something I don't know—which kids love to hear from any adult they invest with authority.

Having long studied several other cultures than our own, psychoanalyst-anthropologist Freeman points to some socio-cultural factors that determine early child development in which truthfulness and lying shape accepted patterns of child rearing. He tells us that in Western culture, autonomy, self-initiation, are prized. "Parents in Western culture have traditionally encouraged their children to become autonomous in looking, thinking, exploring, trying, and discovering . . . and to *not* simply be . . . [puppets that conform, but rather to become their own real person]" (this volume). A Japanese colleague, Freeman tells us, "describes Western culture as 'a culture of nomadism,'" a culture where people move away from the lands of their ancestors.

By contrast, in the Japanese and the Eskimos "parents seek to curtail a growing child's autonomy and to more narrowly channel the child's individuation." There seems to also be more coercion in these two cultures to deceive. For instance, "In Japan, from the time a child . . . becomes part of a school peer group, it is mandatory to consciously pretend and to strictly adhere to a deceptive 'act' . . . in *all* public relationships, . . . to hide . . . inner personal feelings." In one Eskimo culture, Freeman tells us deception plays a serious role in making the child evolve into an adult deemed to better serve society. They do so by means of what the adult world sees as affectionate teasing—rather harsh, I would say—which they put in the service of dwarfing a child's assertiveness linked to autonomy while firming up that which they believe might make the boy a better hunter. And Freeman tells us "that [this] traumatizing and development-arresting [rearing] has survival value for individuals and for the group [given their need to maintain life] in their unusually harsh arctic environment" (this volume).

Can we assume that cultures always evolve for the betterment of their society? I am not an authority in matters of culture, but I have difficulty understanding how this maltreatment of children is in the service of surviving in unusual harsh environmental conditions. Should we assume that if a culture has lived as it has for thousands of years that it has survived because there is wisdom in that culture's mode of surviving? I am not advocating uniformity in cultural child rearing, nor am I suggesting for one moment that our way is the best way, whatever our way may be. Might it be that this Eskimo society, experiencing inordinate pain due to living in such harsh arctic conditions, is externalizing the rage this pain generates in them which they then displace onto their own children? Where there is no dog in the house, the ones to be the last on the 'displacement of rage kicking list' are the children. Even our government is good at it. If funds need to be cut, the first services to be cut are services for children. Of course, my reasoning may be flawed; but does this kind of child rearing indeed have genuine survival value? Should we assume that because a culture has grown over centuries or even millennia to believe that survival in "our given society" requires that children be manipulated and overcontrolled to the point of distorting their natural tendencies that this is in fact to the advantage of the given society?

One has to wonder about the conviction that manipulation and overcontrolling inherent tendencies in children, a conviction that dates back to the beginnings of time, is most advantageous for a society. It seems that Freud's notion that *Homo sapiens* comes into the world a "cauldron of seething excitations" may be a more universal conviction that this is so, given the tendency of the adult world to believe that from early life children must be overcontrolled and manipulated. Yet, just looking at species adjacent to those of *Homo sapiens*, the apes and monkeys hardly seem to give evidence that these magnificently constructed living organisms really behave wildly, raging, tearing each other up, or behaving in a manner destructive or abusive of themselves or others. I insist, having studied children from birth on for nearly four decades that children do not uniformly give evidence of wildly discharging behaviors of any kind. A small percentage of children, those born with an immature central nervous or digestive or respiratory or dermatologic system do. Their thresholds of irritability are low, and the pain their immature system (be it digestive, respiratory, or dermatologic) causes them generates in the high levels of hostile destructiveness which may lead to uncontrollable crying or raging behaviors. In these babies there is an underlying *experiential factor* that leads to their troubling behaviors. Certainly development-optimizing rearing, education, expectations of reasonable behaviors (personal and social), facilitating a child's inborn tendencies is highly desirable. And different cultures have their own measures of what these are. But, it is remarkable how the assumption of wildness, 'original sin,' expectation of scoundrel behavior in newborns, seems to prevail in the adult world. Might it not be in fact, that it is the adult world that behaves this way, as much driven by traumatizing experience as by malfeasant education: "Hate the other because he is not like you and yours," the kernel of "malignant prejudice" (Parens, Mahfouz, Twemlow, and Scharff, 2007)? For now, I shall focus down on more individual aspects of the 'distortion of truth.'

Does the pessimist distort the truth? Does the optimist? Does the optimist distort truth with hope? Does the pessimist distort truth with despair? Is the word 'distort' too strong? A glass that is half full is also half empty. Neither is a distortion of the truth. It's just a matter of which has the greater impact on us. Perhaps that is what the pessimist and the optimist do; they do not distort; they just see the half-reality of their choice. Or is it of their choice?

The distortion of truth, to modify slightly Fischer's observation in quoting M. Kakutani's review of Tobias Wolff's *Our Story Begins* (Fischer, this volume), arises from people's need to cope with the challenges of daily existence. From birth on life's challenges—from being hungry to feeling fear, being bewildered or enraged—make demands on the self to cope. In contrast to 'resilience'—the subject of the 2007 M. S. Mahler Symposium (see Parens, Blum, and Akhtar, 2008)—to which we often respond with admiration, dishonesty, lying, and inauthenticity[1] are not admired, except in perversion and antisociality. But we proceed with caution here, given that when it comes to some lies, for instance, the "Janus Dilemma" prevails, which is that "like with malignant prejudice, the terrorist's action, viewed by the victim as a crime against humanity, is seen by the perpetrator as an act of valor, of honor" (Parens, 2007, p. 288). Thus, while many of us are outraged, many militant anti-Semites applaud Ahmendinijad's denial of the Holocaust.

As the other authors in this book have observed, 'distortions of truth' cover a wide range of human behaviors, from benign 'lying' by omission, as Stone (this volume) notes, or as in lying games[2] and in white lies, to its extreme in rationalizations for mass murder. Beyond the broader view provided by Daniel Freeman, the authors explore 'distortions of truth' in various contexts such as: developmentally, as Ruth Fischer does; clinically, as Lucy La-Farge does; and when carried to extreme in society as Michael Stone does. I will extend the views presented by Stone by adding some of my thoughts, again but further about cultural and social implementations of 'distortion of truth,' especially that put in the service of genocide.

I want to explore 'distortions of truth' along several intertwining parameters: (1) From unconscious to conscious; which melds into the following, (2) From its varying aims, that is, to protect the self; to protect one or more loved ones; to intentionally want to hurt another/others; which has corollaries to, (3) From benign to malignant intent and behavior.

From Conscious to Unconscious

People's need to cope with challenges of everyday life is ever present. The sources of these challenges lie in the large domains of our own psychic activities, as our wishes and our impulses, especially those that are transgressive; the stresses and strains visited on us by our intrapsychic conflicts; the dictates of our conscience; the demands of our narcissism, to repair its injuries or to aggrandize our self-concept, and more. From early in life, toward making survival bearable, it is adaptive to displace, to deny, to avoid, or to repress wishes and impulses arising from within or reactive to external events. For instance, "[twelve-month-old] Jane was visibly angry with her mother. In a moment of heat, Jane picked up a 2 inch wood letter block, raised her arm and flung it, not at her mother but rather at the woman sitting next to her mother. Was her aim poor? I did not think so. Angry with the mother to whom she was already so positively attached, she shifted her aim, and discharged her anger against the woman sitting *next* to mother. Twelve-month-old Jane simply *displaced* the hostility she felt toward her mother, onto someone close by" (Parens, 2007, p 82).

Here is an example taken from longitudinal observational research (Parens, 1979) that gives evidence of *why such defenses are erected*. Thirteen-month-old Mary and her mother had gotten into a series of troubled interactions arising from Mary's wanting to explore a cleaning cart which her mother reasonably disallowed. This morning they got into a battle royal. I conclude the following description of what took place: "For the first time, Mother could not calm Mary as she had quite easily done so many times. Whether Mother held Mary or tried to put her down, Mary's crying and manifest hostility continued . . . Mary physically rejected any efforts Mother made to reduce her distress. Once her crying stopped, Mary's affect was sober and serious. She sat on Mother's lap, erect, as if frozen at the edge of her knees, resisting Mother's gentle efforts to bring her close and sharply complaining when Mother tried to help her. After about 15 minutes in this state of immobilization, Mary's body tone gradually softened, she relaxed passively into her mother's body, thumb in mouth, and stayed there, awake, pensive and downcast for twenty to thirty minutes more" (see Parens, 1979, pp. 202–210 for details of the inferences we drew from this event). In brief, we inferred that Mary's ego (adaptive functions) was paralyzed, unable to resolve the conflicting feelings of wanting to rage at and harm the mother to whom she was so well attached. Her ego, unable to invoke defenses to protect Mary against the intense anxiety generated in her by this high-pitched conflict, was immobilized, suspended in time, for twenty minutes unable to move. Psychoanalysis 101: Defenses are erected to abate painful and excessive anxiety lest the experience become traumatic. From the second half of the first year of life, such self-protective strategies that disallow the thrust of the truth and reality are visibly put into play. More extreme experiences lead to more challenging and personality structuring defenses such as projection, splitting, dissociation, and so forth.

Such defenses, from the benign, as *displacement, avoidance,* and *denial,* to the more moderate *repression,* and the harsher defenses such as *projection, splitting* and *dissociation* occur predominantly *unconsciously.* But some of these may also occur *consciously.* This is especially so with *denial, displacement, suppression,* and a cluster of defenses whose exact intention is to distort the truth. I have proposed that these are especially used in the service of malignant prejudice: *defenses specifically intended to distort reality* include among others *reductionism, caricaturing, depreciation,* and *vilification.* These are often coupled with *generalization.* More on this below.

Interwoven with the *unconscious* and *conscious* parameters of 'distortion of truth' are its varying aims, that is, *to protect the self; to protect one or more loved ones; to wish to intentionally hurt another/others.* Clearly, unconscious use of truth distortion is preponderantly in the service of self-protection; the integrity of the ego and the compliance with emerging superego dictates have a degree of imperative in coping with everyday life. Mary's ego was paralyzed.

Jane's use of displacement was self-protective; but was there some element of to-be-superego factor already operative in twelve-month-old Jane? I have described how one sees the less than one-year-old child internalize maternal dictates, "Don't do that, Jane" her mother repeated, and we saw Jane teasing her mother but complying with that dictate. I joined Spitz (1965) in suggesting that superego precursors begin to be evident from the end of year one (Parens, 1979 [2008], pp. 11, 189–191). It is especially in the domain of conscious behavior that distortion of truth takes the form of what we generally consider to be *lying*, deception, *imposture*, *propaganda*, and so forth.

Various Aims and Targets of Distortion of Reality and Truth

To Protect the Self: In Children

In a recent issue of *New York,* a lay magazine, journalist Po Bronson headlines his article with "Kids lie early, often and for all sorts of reasons—to avoid punishment, to bond with friends, to gain a sense of control" (2008, *New York,* p. 34). Reporting on the work of Nancy Darling, then of Penn State, Bronson asks: "So when do the 98 percent [of kids] who think lying is wrong become the 98 percent who lie" (p. 36)? Essentially this lying is in the service of protecting oneself, to retain the approval of those whose love we need and value while at the same time maintaining a sense of autonomy as one navigates the vicissitudes of everyday life. Telling the lay universe what professionals have learned, for example, Ruth Fischer's and Gail Edelsohn's chapters (this volume), journalist Bronson tells the reader that "It starts very young. Indeed, bright kids . . . are able to start lying at two or three. 'Lying is related to intelligence,' explains Dr. Victoria Talwar, . . . at Montreal's McGill University" (Bronson, p. 36). Ruth Fischer tells us about this.

In a chapter destined to be a classic in psychoanalytic development theory, Fischer lays out the complex developmental weaving of psychic functions that make lying possible. Infants do not come into the world able to lie; they have not yet developed the ego functional ability to do so. Focusing on the level of psychic development that makes lying possible, Fischer suggests that it is "a developmental achievement." Talwar does too (see Bronson, p. 36). Fischer asks, "when [are children] capable of lying and what are the intra-psychic capacities required [to do so]" (p. 2)? Speaking of Freud's (1909) Little Hans, whose fantasies and lies about his little sister Hanna were quite creative, Fischer notes that Freud (1909) first suggested that Little Hans lied in revenge for his father's fabrications about the stork and that he later (1913) added the observation that children lie in imitation, perhaps even in identification with their parents who lie to them. This, interestingly, is the principal thesis of the 2008 lay article by Bronson who probably was not aware of Freud's 1913 observation nearly one hundred years ago.

In her listing the intrapsychic capabilities required for lying, Fischer notes first the evolving establishment of an attachment. Reviewing the process of attachment, she details major findings and ideas from attachment theory itself, as well as those of some key neurobiologists and infant researchers, taking note of the fact that their findings have been observed and written about in substantial detail by an impressive list of psychoanalytic infant observers-theorists. The more recent findings, especially those from neurobiology, are stunning and refreshingly support and even confirm much of the major earlier psychoanalytic findings on the question, theoretical disagreements notwithstanding (some perhaps enlarged and unnecessarily set in competition by individual narcissism like that which drove the Anna Freud vs. John Bowlby debacle of 1960 [see the four opening papers in the *Psychoanalytic Study of the Child*, 1960]).

Juxtaposed to, and perhaps I should say within, the frame of attachment,[3] Fischer follows Mahler's detailing of the process of not only attachment but of the simultaneous evolving of the self in relation to the object of attachment. Fischer suggests that a prerequisite for being able to lie requires that the separation-individuation process has evolved into the child's achievement of a sufficiently structured sense of self and of the object, she suggests during the rapprochement subphase. I would push the developmental subphase a bit further, into the subphase 'on the way to self and object constancy.' My reasoning on this is that the attainment of the child's ability to acknowledge that mother is mother and the child is the child informs us of a level of self and object conceptualization and representation that are acknowledged as stabilizing. As one of our project subjects said to her mother during this latter era of development, "I am Candy, and you are Jeanie," pointing to herself and to her mother in turn as she said their names.

Relying on her strong base knowledge of psychoanalytic developmental theory, Fischer also updates the work of Mahler while she brings her work to bear on the question of lying and deception. Thus, while asserting the explanatory value of Mahler's separation-individuation theory, Fischer has doubts about and puts aside, as others have, Mahler's earlier formulations about the 'autistic phase': "we now appreciate the infant's more independent center of initiative and responsiveness than that which Mahler originally postulated . . . [while] we are focusing with greater interest . . . on the very mother infant interaction that was central to her work" (p. 5). In addition to noting some of Winnicott's thoughts on play (1971), Fischer also notes his contribution to our understanding the child's developing his sense of self

(Winnicott, 1965). She also weaves in P. Tyson's (1996) conceptualization in greater detail of Mahler's concept of 'object constancy.'[4] Tyson, as Fischer says, "[integrates] cognitive and psychoanalytic milestones" in describing her view that object constancy evolves in three stages.

Fischer addressed singularly well each strand of this luxurious fabric of developmental achievements that allow for the complicated behavior of lying and deceiving:

(1) attachment
(2) a demarcated internalized sense of self and other
(3) Mahler's rapprochement subphase
(4) Tyson's representational object constancy
(5) reflective functioning
(6) enhanced affect containment
(7) the ability to play

Especially well done is her discussion of the development of 'the ability to play,' tracing it from its beginnings in the 'transitional space' (Winnicott, 1953) into its richly evolved psychic organization thrust into formation by the child's Oedipus complex, the eighth of these strands of development. The clinical illustrations that accompany Fischer's thoughts are not only charming, but affirming of her theoretical elaborations. Essentially then, Fischer has detailed the complex developmental capabilities and functions needed for a child to become able to 'play' with and distort the truth; it's not all bad.

To Protect the Self: In Adults

In everyday life we also encounter adults, some even well advanced in years who lie, again to protect the self's integrity. A ninety-two-year-old woman has long advised those in her environment that when she is ill, if it's serious she does not want to be told that this is the case. Diagnosed six months before with cancer of the lung with two sites of metastasis she has been treated with chemotherapy and she now believes she is free from cancer! No one is telling her she is not. The regard she has attained in her family has earned her this 'privilege.'

Also in a more serious vein, in our clinical work, we only too commonly encounter human beings whose life has been burdened by the by-product of distortions of truth that arise from the need to protect, to maintain the integrity of their sense of self, to cope with experiences that have, and in many cases continue to challenge their psychic survival. Lucy LaFarge has "linked different forms of deception with different levels of psychic organization" (this volume). Here, as elsewhere, she has detailed some of her efforts to understand and to achieve the arduous work that comes with treating human beings evidencing significant pathology of narcissism.

Having much clinical experience with narcissistic personality disordered patients LaFarge examines the play of deception she has found in treating them. She documents some of the challenges they tend to present in navigating the Kantian uncertainty of what, in what her patients tell her they experienced, corresponds to actual reality. Of course, as I noted before, much of what we experience, our patients and we ourselves, is subjective and with this brings the likelihood of some, even if benign, distortion of truth. But from LaFarge's troubled patients, one can infer that their past has been such that they evoked much fantasy in the service of coping with what one might assume must have been substantial traumatizing interpersonal reality. "For narcissistic patients [she tells us] fantasies of the imaginer [*How* does my parent imagine me? How does my analyst?] and the imagined [*What* does my parent/my analyst imagine of me (child/patient)?] are prominent; and they tend to be highly distorted; often they are split" (this volume, p. 150). What the child (patient) imagines the parent (analyst in the transference) experiences is powerful, be it positive, or be it negatively shaped with neglect or hostility. Indeed, LaFarge notes that "the deceiver [is especially challenged in his or her efforts to cope with, to bring together and manage] wishes and conflicts surrounding *the experience of self* and *the relations of self to reality*, and *the vicissitudes of aggression*" (this volume, italics added). Aggression, more specifically as I have emphasized, hostile destructiveness (Parens, 1979, [2008])—of dimensions corresponding to a cluster of parameters determined by the self's dispositions, object relations, past history, and the traumatizing conditions—gets reactively generated in the self and plays its central part in one's coping with the experience of being and/or having been traumatized, be the trauma *passive* (e.g., neglect) or *active* (e.g., physical, emotional, or sexual abuse).

Her work with such narcissistic patients has led LaFarge to note that the dynamics of deception in the individual vary along a continuum corresponding to dynamics of certain forms of narcissistic disorder. We should note that in these patients, both unconscious and conscious distortions of truth occur. She notes that deception is not always a part of the dynamics of narcissistic personality disordered patients, that "at one end we can locate the group of *non-deceptive* narcissistic patients for whom the [fantasies are for the most part in the service] of *authentication*." In this group of nondeceptive narcissistic patients one encounters various degrees of disturbance and there-

with, however, more distortion of the reality of self and object in the transference and enlarging countertransference challenges. Into the more outright
distorters of truth, LaFarge has found patients who use *imposture* in their ar-
senal of coping mechanisms, in which the patient maintains a split fantasy of
self on the positive side and the parent/analyst on the negative side. Most serious, are the narcissistic patients whose distortion of truth is singularly sadistic; LaFarge speaks of their distortions as *"malicious deception."* This "patient
is primarily identified with the hostile annihilating imagining parent on the
[hostile] side of the split, placing the object [parent/analyst] in the role of a
helpless, annihilated imagined child" (this volume). As with most efforts to
clarify and categorize in our field, lines of demarcation are fuzzy and behaviors shift from one category to another. LaFarge's experience in working with
deceptive patients renders her pessimistic. She earmarks this to be especially
the case with those patients in whom "identification with . . . the aggressively
imagining parent" is dominant. Some of my clinical experience supports La-
Farge's assertion.

Distortions of Truth to Protect A Loved One or Others

May 1940, a Jewish mother and her eleven year-old son, escaping the invading German army on a train from Belgium to southern France are traversing
the region of Dunkirk. They hear explosions that are alarmingly near. Driven
by the impulse to protect her son, eleven, but to her still 'her child,' the
mother spontaneously says, "Don't be frightened, it's only thunder." Appreciating her motherly protectiveness, the son smiles at her. Ten minutes later,
the train stops and they are told to immediately disembark; within moments
of having done so and taken shelter behind dunes, fighter planes strafe the
train, causing little damage. They reembark when told to do so. In an unspoken *entente*, not a word was said about the mother's motherly effort to protect her son against too much fear.

A much more challenging, hazardous, and brazen example is portrayed
movingly in *Life is Beautiful*, a film seen by many several years ago. In it, an
(Italian) father and his perhaps six-year-old son are incarcerated in a Nazi
concentration camp. In a fable-like tale, to protect his son from the horror
they are facing and against the fear experienced by all the incarcerated—as if
fear is not terribly contagious (but this film is a fable)—, the father fabricates
a ruse. As an Italian he volunteers to be the translator for the German officer
commanding their barrack—who does not understand a word of Italian—and
he convinces his young son, in his translations of the orders given, that they
are all engaged in sport games and that he, the youngster is a member of the

team that must do given tasks to earn points. At serious peril to his life, and his son's, the father distorts the truth and the reality they are living through, sparing his son the dread of their life for a precious few weeks. Eventually he is discovered and murdered. The fate of the child is not disclosed. Lies to protect loved ones cannot be maligned, especially when they are created to make life bearable. In wide contrast, what follows can.

The Distortion of Truth with the Intention to Hurt Others

Unfortunately, as is well known, distortion of truth is only too commonly used to hurt another or others. The goal in the intention to hurt another has a wide range, from teasing, to insulting, to blaming, to vilifying. While intention operates unconsciously too, such as the use of defenses to protect oneself, *the intention to hurt others tends to operate predominantly consciously.* When eight-year-old Sammy, made anxious by the fact that he likes Suzie chants "Suzie ha-as cooties!" he teases and may even manage to insult Suzie who in fact does not have "cooties" but whose age-adequate self-esteem is quite vulnerable. And when sixteen year-old Richard fabricates the lie that he "made out" with Rhoda, the prettiest 10th grader with whom he has never been alone, he falsely tries to enhance his self-esteem at the risk of creating a rumor that, if circulated might painfully insult Rhoda. I will address the intentional harming of others that comes with blaming and vilifying below.

Distortions of Truth: From Benign to Malignant Intent

Destructive Distortion of Truth as the Subject of Comedy

Much theater survives on inventive distortions of truth; even some operas do. One addresses this point squarely. In *The Barber of Seville*, opera composer Gioacchino Rossini speaks through the voice of Don Basilio (the music master) who tells Don Bartolo (the aging doctor)—who lusts for the fortune of his pretty ward Rosina who is then falling in love with Count Almaviva—that a strategy for discouraging Rosina's interest in Almaviva is to start a rumor about the count. Rossini does not even suggest what kind of rumor, just a rumor, *una calumnia* (slander, calumny). The magnificent aria *La Calumnia* describes verbally and musically how the rumor starts softly and spreads and gets louder by the bar. It is humor at its best (sung in a comico-conspiratorial tone by a basso); it invariably gets a strong ovation. From humor, the distortion of truth about another takes on a very different meaning when it shifts to insult, and progressively becomes more destructive.

Destructive Distortion of Truth in Severe Character Pathology

Michael Stone has looked at and worked with clinical cases where distortion of truth and reality targeting others is a decisive factor in the conduct of their life. Some were of such startling character that they drew his interest and took him out of the consultation room, therewith widening the arena of our understanding of the play of distortions of truth in severely disturbed individuals, in how it contributes to the dynamics of their criminality. Stone notes that psychoanalysts' awareness that distortions of truth may give rise to antisocial behavior goes back to August Aichhorn (1944), whose classic *Wayward Youth*, first published in 1925, opened the door to psychoanalysis' interest in understanding the path to criminality. Choosing, consciously and unconsciously, to take this path has been explored through studies carried out by analysts besides Aichhorn, by Bowlby on thieves (1946), by Eissler in general (1949), by Schmideberg with adolescent girls (1959), and most recently by James Gilligan with prisoners on death row (1997). There is consensus that its psychic genesis lies in traumatization at the hands of their own families.

Stone tells us of his work as he put it "with two broad groups: borderline, antisocial, and psychopathic patients, and also . . . with mentally-ill offenders and with violent prisoners." He too tries to shed light on at least what he considers to be lying and deceitfulness—that both are "deliberate, fully conscious intention of telling something that is . . .untrue." He reminds us of "Clinton's famous assertion that there may have been fellatio, but there was no sex" (this volume). Among his borderline, antisocial, and psychopathic patients, the pathology is marked, their histories from quite early in life laden with neglect as well as painful, inappropriate, confusing behaviors on the part of the parents, siblings, or other family members; and their behaviors in treatment revealed by their own behaviors what they were accustomed to live with. Lying and deceitfulness were integral in the life they had lived at home, then later in society, and then, quite expectably was brought into their transference behaviors. Stone did not limit his interventional strategies to psychodynamic interventions; his effort to help them took him into the realm of behavior modifications, demand for compliance or dismissal from treatment, social interventions, and even cooperation with authorities to impose compliance on his very troubled patients. His patients' treatment outcome is very mixed, a common experience among quite competent and skilled clinicians and well-committed social agencies. Stone's varied efforts to help could in itself constitute a study of the degree of difficulty encountered in helping such disturbed patients, reflective of the results reported by various disciplines in society—medical, social services, law enforce-ment, legal—that have tried to address the plight of these individuals. Stone, by the way, well illustrates that the problem patients he attempted to treat came from all economic levels of society, a fact well-known in mental health and sociology for decades.

Stone's forensic work has taken him into realms of human behavior where lying and deceitfulness take on ugly dimensions. Violent psychopaths, the extremes of personality disorder, as Stone refers to them, are driven to their severely disordered behavior by distortions of truth and reality that meta-morphose any semblance of reasonableness into irrational, incomprehensible conviction. Their reasoning is not psychotic, not fragmented; it is just a shocking distortion of how things have been, are, and are likely to continue to be. True, there does seem to be an absence of logical judgment; it is a *bizarre* distortion of truth and reality.

Distortions of Truth That Go Beyond Individual Psychology

Michael Stone's cases, disturbing as they are, are individuals who wreak havoc in their own, individual universe; their reach, tragic as it is to their victims' universe, is limited. But when the victim and his/her universe is multiplied manyfold this attains a different level of concern. Indeed, the dis-tortion of truth achieves its greatest potential harm when it is brought into the domain of mass psychology, as in public policy, at the level of societies, nations, ethnic groups, and religious populations. History, from the 6000 years back that it has been recorded is laden with such intentional harming of others. In recent history it is transparent.

During the past one hundred years heads of states have strained the limits of distortion of truth to create such intentional destruction of others. It bears on the question of morality. As I noted at the outset, Holocaust deniers, of which there have been many, are now championed by Ahmadinejad, the President of Iran, who also insists that the Holocaust is a fabrication and that the truth about Jews lies in *The Protocols of the Elders of Zion*. Middle Eastern radio and television have recently intoned the same distortion and sup-planted the truth about the Holocaust with airings of *The Protocols*. Brenner, who has researched its origins reports that *The Protocols of the Elders of Zion* "is a document of about 100 pages [after all, for the masses it should not be too long] containing twenty-four chapters that describe a secret Jewish con-spiracy for world domination. [The document was created in 1898 by] Math-ieu Golovinski, a known plagiarist . . . in order to frame the enemies of the czarist government. [He] was in the employ . . . of the czarist police" (Bren-ner, 2007, p. 156). Brenner tells us that it was a modification with references to Jews of a "parable written . . . in 1864 by Maurice Joly . . . to incite the masses against the tyrannical rule of Napoleon III of France . . . . First published in Germany in 1919, it was quickly embraced by Hitler . . . . Despite court decisions . . . denouncing the *Protocols* as a fake in 1937, it [has] continued to be published and distributed in [various countries into this century]" (p. 156–157). I shall return to Hitler's use of *The Protocols*.

Our heads of state believed, asserting they had evidence, that Saddam Hussein had been stockpiling weapons of mass destruction. U.S. National Intelligence gathering for all intents and purposes supported this declaration. Our heads of state, in collaboration with some other sovereign states, launched a war against Iraq. After many deaths on both sides of the conflict, no weapons of mass destruction were found. This war continues. What did our intelligence agencies know? Not know? Feared was there? Wished was there? How much was a dedicated search for truth? We may never know whether the supposed truth: 'Saddam Hussein has weapons of mass destruction,' was truly believed or was manufactured to serve a hidden imperative.

Distortion of Truth as an Attack on Morality and a Crime Against Humanity

Rossini's *La Calumnia* is a distortion of truth aimed at harming another. But it is humor. Possibly the most grievous types of destructive distortion of truth which has been an attack on morality were developed by the heads of state of Germany's Third Reich. Two such types of distortions of truth were used: a highly sophisticated, abominable *propaganda* and a government programmed set of outright *deceptions*.

Propaganda
Between 1933 and 1938, legalized in 1935 in what came to be known as *The Nuremberg Laws*, Jews were denied their previously held right to German citizenship, to all the major professions, to hold public office, attend public schools, even to shop in German stores. These legal degradations laid the groundwork for the propaganda. Given that to the Nazi government of Germany these anti-Semitic laws[5] against its own citizens did not seem to go far enough, this government developed a devastating propaganda machine: the ultimate in destructive distortion of truth in the civilized Western world.

Propaganda in The Third Reich was of such priority that it was organized into a ministry; Joseph Goebbels was its minister. According to Saul

Friedlander (2007), "On November 2 [1939] . . . the propaganda minister [Goebbels] told Hitler . . . that anti-Jewish propaganda . . . ought to be substantially reinforced: 'We consider . . . whether we shouldn't stress the Zionist Protocols [sic][6] (The Protocols of the Elders of Zion) in our propaganda in France.' The use of the 'Protocols' was to reappear in Goebbels' plans throughout the war, mainly toward the end. More than once he would discuss this issue with Hitler" (Friedlander, 2007, p. 19). Goebbels was not the only gifted propagandist during Hitler's dramatically aborted "1000 year Reich." Goebbels' subordinate Otto Dietrich was as virulent. He asserted that "the battle against the Jewish and reactionary war mongers . . . who wish to salvage their exploitation methods through this war . . . [is] a part of the daily press material. . . . Only with closest attention on the part of the [newspaper] editors to stressing Jewish capitalist themes will the necessary long-term propagandist effect be achieved" (Friedlander, 2007, p. 23). And akin to the 'Protocols,' Robert Ley, a Nazi party leader, had his own magnified distortions. Quoting Friedlander, "For him . . . Jewish plutocracy was 'the dominance of money and gold, the repression and enslavement of people, the reversal of all natural values and exclusion of reason and insight; the mystical darkness of superstition . . . the meanness of human carnality and brutality.' No common ground existed between this evil and the good that the National Socialist Volksgemeischaft [community]" (pp. 23–24).

The Third Reich's Programmed Deceptions

The first of these is Kristallnacht. According to William Shirer (1960), on November 7, 1938, Herschel Grynszpan, a seventeen-year-old German Jewish refugee, shot and mortally wounded the third secretary of the German Embassy in Paris. His father "had been among ten thousand Jews deported to Poland in boxcars [during that early time they were only expelling Jews from Germany to the East, they were not yet murdering them] . . . and it was to revenge this and the general persecution of Jews in Nazi Germany that he went to the German Embassy intending to kill the ambassador, Count Johannes von Welczeck. But the young third secretary was sent out to see what he wanted, and was shot" (Shirer, 1960, p. 430). Then, "on the night of November 9-10 . . . the worst pogrom that had yet taken place in Germany occurred. . . . According to Goebbels and the German press . . . it was a 'spontaneous' . . . demonstration of the German people in reaction to the news of the murder in Paris. . . . After the war, documents came to light which show how 'spontaneous' it was. They are among the most illuminating—and gruesome—secret papers of the prewar Nazi era" (p. 430).

On the evening of November 9, according to a secret report made by the chief party judge, Major Walther Buch, Goebbels issued instructions that "spontaneous demonstrations" were to be "organized and executed" during the night. . . . The real organizer was Reinhard Heydrich, the sinister 34-year-old number two man of the SS. His teletyped orders . . . are among the captured German documents.

a. Only measures should be taken which do not involve danger to German life or property. (For instance, synagogues are to be burned down only when there is no danger of fire to the surroundings.)
b. Business and private apartments of Jews may be destroyed but not looted. . . .
c. The demonstrations that are going to take place should not be hindered by the police. . . .
>   1. As many Jews, especially rich ones, are to be arrested as can be accommodated in the existing prisons. . . . Upon their arrest, the appropriate concentration camps should be contacted immediately, in order to confine them in these camps as soon as possible.

(Shirer, 1960, pp. 430–431)

The elaborate orders, the directness of the deception, the dimensions of the criminality of Goebbels' lie, are a matter of history. It was only the prelude of what would become the "Final Solution" which was put into action soon after it was officially stated and recorded on January 20, 1942. The second major deception perpetrated by the Third Reich was the assertion made to Jews, Romas (Gypsies), and others similarly selected, that they were (forcibly) assembled for relocation to areas East (of Europe) where they would be put to work. In fact, they were relocated to what eventually became the death camps and most were murdered. "Relocation" soon became known to mean to the death camps.

The distortion of truth and of reality has its place in our life, for better and for worse.

Notes

1. I assume that we all agree that in theater and movies acting cannot be construed as inauthenticity. It is an intentional portrayal and is so understood by the audience that applauds this form of life experience representation.
2. A famous 'distortion of truth' game which we played years ago was "Telephone." Among a group of teens in a party setting, one teenager writes a message on a piece of paper. He/she then whispers into the ear of another teen, who whispers the message in the ear of another, and so on until the last hearer of the message is reached

who then writes in on another piece of paper. The messages are then compared to the amusement of all involved.

3. I view the cluster of contributions by Rene Spitz ("the structuring of the libidinal object" [1946, 1965]), John Bowlby (attachment theory [1958, 1969]), and Margaret Mahler, et al. (separation-individuation theory [1975]), together, to be the foremost explanatory theorizing advanced toward our understanding of attachment, minor disagreements notwithstanding.

4. Mahler's concept differs from that detailed by Selma Fraiberg (1969), which speaks to an earlier notion of 'object constancy' as used by Hartmann and Anna Freud. Mahler's concept was, in addition to following Hartmann, more linearly related to Piaget's (concept of 'object permanence') and Spitz's (1965) 'structuring of the libidinal object' with special emphasis on the 'libidinal' aspect of object constancy.

5. Six years later, in October 1940, laws almost identical to the Nuremberg Laws were instituted in war-defeated France by the pro-Nazi Vichy government of 'Free France.'

6. "[sic]" is in the original Friedlander text.

References

Aichhorn, A. (1944). *Wayward Youth*. New York: Viking Press (First German edition, 1925).

Akhtar, S. (1999). *Immigration and Identity: Turmoil, Treatment, and Transformation*. Northvale, NJ: Jason Aronson.

Bowlby, J. (1946). *Forty-Four Juvenile Thieves*. London: Balliere, Tindall & Cox.

Bowlby, J. (1958). The nature of the child's tie to his mother. *International Journal of Psychoanalysis* 39: 350–373.

Bowlby, J. (1969). *Attachment*. New York: Basic Books.

Brenner, I. (2007). Contemporary anti-Semitism: variations of an ancient theme. In: *The Future of Prejudice: Psychoanalysis and the Prevention of Prejudice*, H. Parens, A. Mahfouz, S.W. Twemlow, and D.E. Scharff, ed. Pp. 141–161. Lanham, MD: Rowman & Littlefield Publishers, Inc.

Bronson, B. (2008). Learning to lie. *New Yorker*, February 18, pp. 34–39, 95.

Eissler, K.R. (1949). *Searchlights on Delinquency*. New York: International Universities Press.

Fischer, R.M.S. (2008). What it takes to tell a lie. *This Volume*.

Fraiberg, S. (1969). Libidinal object constancy and mental representation. *Psychoanalytic Study of the Child* 24: 9–47.

Freeman, D. (2009). Socio-cultural perspectives on dishonesty and lying. *This Volume*.

Friedlander, S. (2007). *Nazi Germany and the Jews 1939-1945: The Years of Extermination*. New York: HarperCollins Publishers.

Gilligan, J. (1997). *Violence: Reflections on a National Epidemic.* New York: Vintage Books (G. P. Putnam's Sons, 1996).

LaFarge, L. (2008). Authentication, imposture, and malicious deception. *This Volume.*

Mahler, M.S., Pine, F., and Bergman, A. (1975). *The Psychological Birth of the Human Infant.* New York: Basic Books.

Parens, H. (1979). *The Development of Aggression in Early Childhood.* New York: Jason Aronson. Also in *Revised Edition* (2008).

Parens, H. (2004). *Renewal of Life—Healing from the Holocaust.* Rockville, MD: Schreiber Publishing.

Parens, H. (2007). The roots of prejudice: Findings from observational research. In: *The Future of Prejudice: Psychoanalysis and the Prevention of Prejudice*, ed. H. Parens, A. Mahfouz, S.W. Twemlow, and D.E. Scharff, pp. 81–95. Lanham, MD: Rowman & Littlefield Publishers, Inc.

Parens, H., Blum, H.P., and Akhtar, S., eds. (2008). *The Unbroken Soul—Tragedy, Trauma, and Human Resilience.* New York: Rowman & Littlefield Publishers, Inc.

Parens, H., Mahfouz, A., Twemlow, S.W., and Scharff, D.E., eds. (2007). *The Future of Prejudice: Psychoanalysis and the Prevention of Prejudice.* Lanham, MD: Rowman & Littlefield Publishers, Inc.

Schmideberg, M. (1959). Psychiatric treatment of the female offender. *Correction* 24: 7–8.

Shirer, W. (1960). *The Rise and Fall of the Third Reich.* New York: Simon and Schuster.

Spence, D.P. (1982). *Narrative Truth and Historical Truth. Meaning and Interpretation in Psychoanalysis.* New York: W. W. Norton & Co.

Spitz, R. (1946). The smiling response: a contribution to the ontogenesis of social relations. *Genetic Psychology Monographs* 34: 57–125.

Spitz, R. (1965). *The First Year of Life.* New York: International Universities Press.

Stone, M.H. (2008). Lying and deceitfulness in personality disorders. *This Volume.*

Tyson, P. (1996). Object relations, affect management and psychic structure formation: the concept of object constancy. *Psychoanalytic Study of the Child* 51: 172–189.

Winnicott, D.W. (1953). Transitional objects and transitional phenomena: a study of the first not-me possession. *International Journal of Psychoanalysis* 34: 89–97.

Winnicott, D.W. (1965). *The Maturational Processes and the Facilitating Environment.* London: Hogarth.

Winnicott, D.W. (1971). *Playing and Reality.* London: Tavistock.

Index

Addington, Crandall, 138
adolescence: argument perception of, 40; autonomy and, 38, 62, 94; lying and, 38–39; lying motivation of, 39
adults: lying and, 149–51; self protection of, 149–51
The Adventures of Pinocchio (Collodi), 103
Aichhorn, August, 69, 153
Akhtar, S., 100, 103
Akira Kurosawa, 141
"The Anatomy of Self" (Doi), 134
anger: BPD and, 99; truth distortions, 145–46
antisocial personality disorder, 78–80; definition of, 99; diagnosis of, 100; guilt, lack of, 100; inferiority felt by, 101; lying and, 99–102; lying types and, 101; narcissism and, 100; polygraph and, 106; speech/emotional integration and, 100
Armsden, G.C, 131
art, forgery of, 5
attachment, establishment of, 19–20, 148

authentication, 45; analysis for, 48; clinical vignette on, 46–49; fantasy of, 47–48; self discovery and, 46, 48
"Authentication, Lying, and Malicious Deception" (LaFarge), 59
autonomy: adolescence and, 38, 62, 94; child development and, 142–43; Eskimos and, 116, 120–21; Japanese and, 116; Western culture push for, 116–17

Balint, Michael, 135
Barber, April, 89
Barber, Justin, 89
The Barber of Seville, 152
Bartolo, Don, 152
Basilio, Don, 152
behavioral observation, for deception detection, 103–5
Bion, Wilfred, 4
borderline personality disorder (BPD): abandonment fear and, 98; antisocial features and, 74–78; case one on, 75–76; case three on, 77–78; case two on, 76–77; clinical features of,

~

About the Editors and Contributors

About the Editors and Contributors

Salman Akhtar, M.D., professor of psychiatry, Jefferson Medical College; training and supervising analyst, Psychoanalytic Center of Philadelphia, Philadelphia, PA.

Harold P. Blum, M.D., clinical professor of psychiatry, New York University School of Medicine; training and supervising analyst, New York University Psychoanalytic Institute, New York, NY.

Gail A. Edelsohn, M.D., M.S.P.H., associate medical director, Children's Services, Department of Behavioral Health and Mental Retardation, Philadelphia, PA.

Ruth M.S. Fischer, M.D., clinical professor of psychiatry, University of Pennsylvania School of Medicine; training and supervising analyst, Psychoanalytic Center of Philadelphia, Philadelphia, PA.

Daniel M.A. Freeman, M.D., faculty member, Psychoanalytic Center of Philadelphia, Philadelphia, PA.

Lucy LaFarge, M.D., clinical associate professor of psychiatry, Weil Cornell Medical School; training and supervising analyst, Columbia University Psychoanalytic Center, New York, NY.

Mark Moore, Ph.D., director of psychological services, Joan Karnell Cancer Center, Pennsylvania Hospital, Philadelphia, PA.

Henri Parens, M.D., professor of psychiatry, Jefferson Medical College; training and supervising analyst, Psychoanalytic Center of Philadelphia, Philadelphia, PA.

Michael H. Stone, M.D., professor of clinical psychiatry, Columbia College of Physicians and Surgeons, New York, NY.

Clarence Watson, J.D., M.D., clinical director of forensic services, Delaware Psychiatric Center, New Castle, Delaware; assistant professor of psychiatry, Department of Psychiatry, Jefferson Medical College.